Useful phrases for purchasers (2)

My (our) budget is limited!

Mon (notre) budget est limité!

Have you ... Avez-vous ...

... anything cheaper (less expensive)?
... quelque chose de mois cher?
... at a mid-price? ... à prix modéré?
... at a low-price? ... à bas prix?

I would like (We would like) ...
Je voudrais (nous voudrions)...

... to have help to ... ... avoir aide à ...
... to have advice about ...
... avoir conseils à propos de ...
... to look through the catalogue
... consulter le catalogue
to have a look at ... examiner ...

Can I (we) ...

Est-ce que je peux (nous pouvons) ...

... place an order for ...?
... passer une commande pour ... ?
... have an invoice? ... avoir une facture?

I'll take that! Je prends ça!

Thank you. Merci.

Thank you very much. Merci bien.

Thank you very much indeed.

Merci beaucoup.

Goodbye Au revoir.

(Vendor): *Go*

GW00722431

ii

Will's DIY Dictionary
English – French – English

From Sewage to
Shocking Pink

Compiled, Edited and
Published by
William Rees

Premier (Review) Edition 2008.

© William Rees

Published by:
William Rees
3 Waterloo Terrace,
Carmarthen SA31 1DG
Wales UK

Printed by Book Printing UK
Peterborough

Editor's Introduction.

It happened somewhere between St-Jouin-de-Marnes and Taizé on the D37 just over the border from la Vienne and into Deux-Sèvres. The first village boasts an astonishing 11th century basilica that dominates this part of the great plain of Poitou. At the second a more modest pre-historic dolmen can be found.

Whether influenced by primeval or spiritual forces I know not but on that journey (some years ago now) it occurred to me that my rudimentary French was not the greatest impediment facing me at my destination – one of the *bricolage* stores at nearby Thouars. Indeed divine intervention was not needed to engender the prosaic thought that a knowledge of the subjunctive, the gerund and the past anterior tense were hardly required to buy, say, a sheet of PDF (the DIYer's staple fibreboard). However the information that the French term for the product is *lamifié* could be of considerable assistance in such a quest.

The idea metamorphosed in several guises in the intervening period and grew to encompass more general house and garden terms. *Will's DIY Dictionary* now sees the light of day with the supplementary title **From Sewage to Shocking Pink.** That designation fell off the page by chance when the selection of words falling between the two terms filled a page and provided the 'owl's ears' that typify a dictionary's page.

That providential event effectively defined the principal aim of the volume – to provide a specialist lexicon that will be useful for property holders in France – particularly those with aspirations to improve their homes. It ranges from names to define exotic colour schemes to those that assist with the discharge of detritus!

My hope is that it will be of value to those who find themselves at home in France.

William Rees – Editor

About this book

The aspiration has been to compile a lexicon relevant to establishing and maintaining a home in France. A high percentage of the words listed are specialist terms that will not be found in the average general purpose dictionary. It is hoped that other features will be of assistance to readers.

Inside the front covers there's a list of linking phrases that may facilitate making purchases and placing orders.

Convenience of use has been a guiding principle. It's designed as a pocket-book that will become a helpful companion in the handbag, pocket or glove compartment.

It's overall size is 11 cm x 20 cm and it has the unique feature of having measures in metric and Imperial units printed around the edges of the back cover.

Within the text there are occasional short informative articles. More conversation pieces than instructions they reflect the Editor's experience of life in France. They should not be taken to be definitive of current law and practice at any one time.

Accidents happen in the home – particularly when undertaking maintenance work. There is advice about contacting Emergency Services within the text under both **'Accident'** and **'Emergency'**. In addition there are a range of useful expressions and body-part names inside the back cover.

This volume has been compiled to help people communicate. It is not a language text book. The grammatical information provided is confined to basic word forms with the following abbreviations:
n – noun; v – verb
adj – adjective; adv – adverb
and the occasional *pp – past participle.*
Gender of nouns is indicated by
(m) – male; (f) – female.
Where there are irregular male / female word endings they are shown as follows:
best *n* meilleur (re) *(m)/(f)*
load bearing *adj* porteur (euse) *(m)/(f)*
Irregular noun plural endings are shown as:
stained glass window *n* vitrail (aux) *(m)*
Nouns and adjectives which do not change their spellings for gender or plurality are shown as: *inv*

And finally – TIY – Take It with You!
When stumped at the DIY store there's little point in having *Will's* lying on the lounge table!

Acknowledgements

This wordbook was first conceived some years ago and since then several formats have been considered and more than one hiatus has intervened in its development. Nevertheless none of it would have happened without the assistance of Sara Debrach. As a prime mover Sara, then running her own translation agency in Brive-la-Gaillarde, provided invaluable help and support. Subsequently her husband Francis added weight to our efforts to achieve publication. I thank them both most profoundly. They are currently the *patrons* of the Auberge sur Vézère at St Viance – a much acclaimed hostelry and restaurant a few kilometres outside Brive.

The bulk of the compilation was undertaken after the Editor had returned to live in Wales. He was fortunate to be able to enlist the assistance of long-standing friends Marie-France and Nigel Addinall. Marie-France is a native of Bordeaux and a graduate of that city's university. Nigel gained BA and Ph D degrees at the University of Reading before also graduating in Bordeaux. Both have been members of the French faculty at the University of Swansea for many years. To that Nigel adds the distinction of being the French Honorary Consul for Swansea.

Nigel and Marie-France kindly looked over the first of several 'final' drafts and pointed out many errors. The Editor is indebted to them for their efforts. He must stress that any mistake or misapprehension remaining in the published work is entirely attributable to him (The Editor) – and him alone.

Contents

Omissions.

Readers may find that something they consider to be an invaluable piece of kit or adjunct to the home is not included in this volume. We would be glad to have any such thoughts drawn to our attention so that they may be considered for inclusion in future editions. The Editor can be contacted by e-mail on:
william-rees@tiscali.co.uk

x

abrasive *n* abrasif *(m)*
abrasive paper *n* papier *(m)* abrasif
abrasive stone *n* pierre *(f)* abrasif
AC *n* (elec. current) courant *(m)* alternatif
accelerator *n* (adhesives etc.) accélérateur *(m)*

Accident and Emergency

**Europe wide emergency - ☏ 112
(Access to English speaking operators).
France Medical Assistance ☏ 15**
(In either case use a land-line telephone if
possible so that your call can be easily traced)

**The Europe wide Emergency Telephone
number – 112 should particularly be noted.**
Established under the auspices of the EU
their web-site states: "English interpretation
service available for other foreign languages".
It also reminds us that the location of a caller
using a French land line will be displayed to
the operator within 3 seconds of the call being
accepted. Determining where you are may
take up to 30 minutes if you use a mobile.
(See also Medical Phrases and Body Part terms
inside back cover)

---

accommodation *n* logement *(m)*
account *n* compte *(m)*
accurate *adj* (instrument) juste; (assessment)
correct
acetone *n* acétone *(f)*
acetylene *n* acétylène *(m)*
acid *n* acide *(m)*
acre *n* acre *(f);* (metric equivalent = .405 ha.
(4,050 sq. m.)
acrylic *n* acrylique *(m)*
adapter *n* (elec. connector) adaptateur *(m)*
additive *n* additif *(m)*
adhere (to) *v* adherer

Adhesive

adhesive *n* adhésif *(m);* colle *(f)*

mastic ~ : colle mastic
neoprene ~ : colle neoprene
silicone ~ : colle silicone
waterproof ~ : colle impermeable
wood glue : colle bois

---

adhesive tape *n* papier *(m)* adhésif;
Scotch ® *(m)*
adjoin (to) *v* être contigu (uë) à
adjoining *adj* (building) attenant; (room) voisin
adjustable *adj* (height etc.) réglable
adjustable spanner *n* clé *(f)* à molette
adjustment *n* réglage *(m);* modification *(f)*
adjustment (to make ~ to ...) apporter des
modifications à ....
advice *n* (general) conseils *(mpl)*
advice about .... conseils à propos de . ....
advice note *n* avis *(m)* d'expédition
advice of delivery *n* avis de réception
advice on ... conseils *(mpl)* sur .....
advisor *n* conseiller (ère) *(m)/(f)*
aerial *n* antenne *f)*
aerial *n* **(satellite ~)** antenne *(f)* parabolique
aerosol *n* (spray can) bombe *(f)* aérosol
aerosol paint *n* peinture *(f)* en aérosol
affix (to) *v* coller
aggregate *n* agrégat *(m)*
agitator *n* agitateur *(m)*
aid *n* aide *(f)*
aid to ... aide à ....
air brick *n* brique (f) creuse
air conditioned *adj* climatisé
air conditioning *n* climatisation *(f);* air *(m)*
conditionné
air cylinder *n* **(compressed ~)** cylindre *(m)*
à air comprimé
air duct *n* conduit *(m)* d'air
air valve *n* (central heating) purgeur *(m)* d'air

air vent *n* prise *(f)* d'air
airway *n* (for breathing) voie *(f)* respiratoire
alabaster *n* albâtre *(m)*
alarm *n* alarme *(f)*
(burglar ~) alarme *(f)* contre le vol
(fire ~) alarme *(f)* incendie
(smoke ~) détecteur *(m)* de fumée
alarm bell *n* sonnette *(f)* alarme
alarm clock *n* réveille matin *(m)*
alcove *n* alcôve *(f)*
alder *n* (wood; tree) aulne *(m)*
algaecide *n* algicide *(m)*
alkali *n* alcali *(m)*
alkaline *adj* alcalin
alkalinity *n* alcalinité *(f)*
Allen key *n* clé *(f)* Allen
alter (to) *v* (general) changer; modifier;
(building) transformer
alternating current (AC) *n* courant *(m)*
alternatif
aluminium *n* aluminium *(m)*
aluminium foil *n* papier *(m)* aluminium
ambulance *n* ambulance *(f)*
ammonia *n* ammoniac *(f)*
ammonia-based *adj* ammoniaqué (e)
amp / ampere *n* ampère *(m)*
amplification *n* amplification *(f)*
amplifier *n* amplificateur *(m)*
analyse (to) *v* analyser
analysis *n* analyse *(f)*
analyst *n* analyste *(m)/(f)*
anchor position *n* point *(m)* d'ancrage
anchor ring *n* cigale *(f)*
anchor (to) *v* (awning; roof) arrimer
angle *n* angle *(m)*
angle bracket *n* (flat) équerre *(f)*
angle grinder *n* meuleuse *(f)*
angle iron *n* cornière *(f)*
angle plate *n* équerre *(f)* de montage
angular *adj* (architecture) plein d'angles
annulated / ring shank nail : clou annelé

anode *n* anode *(f)*
answerphone *n* répondeur *(m)* téléphonique
ant *n* fourmi *(f)*
(black ~) fourmi *(f)* noir (commune)
antenna *n* antenne *(f)*
anticorrosive *n* produit *(m)* anticorrosion
anti-humidity *adj* anti-humidité
anti-moss treatment *n* traitement
antimousse *(m)*
anti-return valve *n* clapet *(m)* anti-retour
anti-rust *adj* antirouille
apex *n* sommet *(m)*
appro. *n* **(on ~ , on approval)** à l'essai
approximately *adv* (about, approx.) environ
approximation *n* approximation *(f)*
apron *n* (clothing) tablier *(m);* **(parking ~)** aire
(f) de stationnement
arc lamp *n* lampe *(f)* à arc
arc welder *n* soudeur *(m)* à arc
arc welding *n* soudage *(m)* à arc
arch *n* (archway) arche *(f)*
architect *n* architecte *(m)*
architrave *n* architrave *(f)*
area *n* (of place, item) aire *(f):* (of land)
superficie *(f)*

Area – Conversion table

Imperial Measure (UK) - Metric
1 sq. inch = 6.45 sq. centimetre
1 sq. foot = 0.0929 sq. metre (m.)
1 sq. yard (yd.) = 0.836 sq. m.
1 acre (4840 sq. yd.) = 0.405 hectares (ha.)
(4047 sq. m.)
1 sq mile (640 acres) = 2.59 sq, kilometres
(259 ha.)

Metric - Imperial Measure (UK)
1 sq.centimetre = .155 sq. inch
1 sq. metre (m.) = 10.76 sq. foot
= 1.1960 sq. yard
1 ha. (10,000 sq. m.) = 2.47 acres
1 sq. km (100 ha.) = 0.386 sq. ml (247 acres)

---

asbestos *n* amiante *(m)*
asbestos mat *n* plaque *(f)* d'amiante
asbestosis *n* asbestose *(m)*
ash *n* (result of burning) cendre *(f)*
ash *n* (wood; tree) frêne *(m)*
asphalt *n* bitume *(m)*
assemble (to) *v* assembler
attic *n* grenier *(m)*
attic (habitable ~) grenier *(m)* aménagé
attic room *n* mansarde *(f)*
attic window *n* lucarne *(f)*
auger *n* (for timber) vrille *(f); (in land)* foreuse *(f)*
auto-latch *n* loquet *(m)* automatique
awl *n* alêne *(f)*
awning *n* (house: restaurant) auvent *(m);*
(~ + base support) store *(m)* sur pied
axe *n* hache *(f)*
azure *n/adj* (colour) azur *(m)*

back door *n*   porte *(f)* de derrière
back room *n*   chambre *(f)* du fond
backstairs *npl*   escalier *(m)* de service
backyard *n*   arrière cour *(f)*
bad *n*   mauvais *(m)*
baize *n*   drap *(m)* de billard
Bakelite ® *n*   Bakélite ® *(f)*
balance *n* (scales for weighing)   balance *(f)*
balcony *n*   balcon *(m)*
ball *n* (of clay etc.)   boule *(f);* (of string) pelote *(f)*
ball and socket joint *n*   joint *(m)* à rotule
ball shaped *adj*   en forme de balle
ball valve *n*   vanne *(f)*
balustrade *n*   balustrade *(f)*
bamboo *n* (plant, wood)   bambou *(m)*
band *n* (rubber / elastic)   bande *(f)* élastique
band saw *n*   scie *(f)* à ruban
banister *n* (handrail)   rampe *(f)*
bar *n* (rod of metal / wood)   barre *(f);* barreau *(m)*
barbed *adj* (spikes, thorns)   à barbes
barbed wire *n*   fil *(m)* de fer barbelé
bare *adj* (blade, wood, wire)   nu
barn *n*   grange *(f)*
bars *npl* (on window)   grille *(f)*
base *n* (gen.)   base *(f);* (of a fitting, appliance) socle *(m)*
base board *n*   plinthe *(f)*
basement *n*   sous sol *(m)*
basin *n* (bowl)   bol *(m);* (for personal washing) lavabo *(m)*
basket *n* (with handle)   panier *(m)*
bas relief *n*   bas relief *(m)*
bat *n* (flying animal)   chauve souris *(f)*
bath *n* (water, chemical)   bain *(m);* (sanitary equipment) baignoire *(f)*
bath (to) *v*   baigner
bath mat *n*   tapis *(m)* de bain
bathroom *n*   salle *(f)* de bains
bathroom cabinet *n*   armoire *(f)* de toilette
bathroom fittings *npl*   accessoires *(mpl)* de bain

bathroom scales *npl* pèse personne *(m)*; balance (f)
bathtub *n* baignoire *(f)*
batten *n* (for door, floor) latte *(f);* (roofing) volige *(f)*
battery *n* (small appliances) pile *(f);* (car, vehicles) batterie *(f)*
battery acid *n* solution *(f)* acide pour piles
battery charger *n* chargeur *(m)* de batteries
bay window *n* bow window *(m);* oriel *(m)*
beading *n* (wood or plastic strips) baguette *(f);* (as a decoration on a surface) chapelet *(m)*
beam *n* poutre *(f)*
beam balance *n* balance *(f)* à fléau
bed *n* lit *(m)*
bed base *n* sommier *(m)*
bedroom *n* chambre *(f)* (à coucher)
bedroom furniture *npl* meubles *(fpl)* de chambre à coucher
beech *n* (tree; wood) hêtre *(m)*
beetle *n* scarabée *(f);* **(death watch ~ ; furniture ~)** vrillette *(f)*
beige *n/adj* (colour) beige *(m)*
bell *n* (chiming) cloche *(f);* (door, buzzer) sonnette *(f)*
bell wire *n* câble *(m)* paire parallèle
bench *n* (workbench) établi *(m)*
bench lathe *n* tour *(m)* à banc
bench seat *n* banquette *(f)*
bend *n* (in pipework) coude *(m)*
bend *n* (U-~) coude *(m)* en U
bend (to make a ~ in ...) *v* (pipe) faire un coude à ...
bend (to) *v* (pipes) cintrer; (wire) plier
bending spring *n* (plumbing) ressort *(m)* à cintrer
best *n* meilleur (re) *(m)/(f)*
better *n* mieux *inv*
bevel *n* biseau *(m)*
bevel (to) *v* (an edge e.g. mirror) tailler en biseau

Bevelled mirror   **Bolt**

bevelled mirror *n* glace *(f)* biseautée
bidet *n* bidet *(m)*
big *adj* grand
bill *n* (Invoice) facture *(f)*
bin liner *n* sac *(m)* poubelle
birch *n* (wood, tree) bouleau *(m)*
bit *n* (for drill i.e. the cutting ~) mèche *(f)*
bitumen *n* bitume *(m)*
black *n/adj* (colour) noir *(m);* **(jet ~)** *n* noir
(m) d'ébène
blacksmith *n* forgeron *(m)*
black ant *n* fourmi *(f)* noir (commune)
blade *n* (knife; tool) lame *(f);* **blade** (of fan,
propeller) pale *(f)*
blade of... lame de …
bleach *n* eau *(f)* de javel
bleach (to) *v* blanchir
bleed valve *n* robinet *(m)* de purge
blind *n* (window) store *(m);* **(roller ~)** store
enroulé *(m);* **(Venetian ~)** store vénitien *(m)*
block *n* (slab) bloc *(m);*
(concrete ~) bloc (m) de béton
(hollow concrete ~) bloc (m) de beton creux
block and tackle *n* moufle *(f)*
block board *n* latté *(m)*
blockage *n* (in pipe, gutter etc) blocage *(m)*
blowlamp: blowtorch *n* chalumeau *(m);*
lampe *(f)* à souder
blue *n/adj* (colour) bleu *(m)*
blunt *adj* (knife, chisel) émoussé
blunt (to) *v* émousser
board *n* (plank) planche *(f);* (panel) panneau
(m); **(skirting ~)** plinthe *(f)*
boards *npl* **(floor ~)** plancher *(m)*
boiler *n* (heating) chaudière *(f)*
boiler suit *n* (working clothes) bleu *(m)* de
travail
bolster *n* (bricklayer's chisel) ciseau (x) *(m)* de
briqueteur
bolt *n* (with screw thread) boulon *(m);* (lock)
verrou *(m)*

bolt (to) *v* (fix items together) boulonner;
(lock) verrouiller
bolt cutters *npl* coupe boulons *(mpl)*
bond *n* adhérence *(f); liaison (f)*
bottle *n* bouteille *(f)*
bottom *n* fond *(m)*
boundary *n* limite *(f)* du terrain
bowl *n* cuvette *(f)*
box *n* (small) boîte *(f);* (larger) caisse *(f)*
box room *n* débarras *(m)*
brace *n* (hold up) support *(m)*
brace (to) *v* (wall; structure) renforcer:
consolider
brace and bit *n* vilebrequin *(m)*
bracket *n* (for shelf) équerre *(f)*
brad *n* (floor nail) clou *(m)* à tête perdue;
clou *(m)* sans tête
bradawl *n* tarière *(f)* à gouge
brass *n* (metal) laiton *(m)*; cuivre *(m)* jaune
brass *n* **(the ~)** (ornaments etc.) cuivres *(mpl)*
braze *v* (hard solder) braser
breadth *n* largeur *(f)*
breathing *n* respiration *(f)*
breeze block *n* parpaing *(m)*
(hollow ~) parpaing *(m)* creux
(lightweight ~) parpaing *(m)* cellulaire
brick *n* brique *(f)*
brick up (to) *v* (fireplace; door) murer;
(hole) boucher
bricklayer *n* briqueteur *(m)*
bricklayer's chisel *n* (bolster) ciseau (x) *(m)*
de briqueteur
bricklayer's trowel *n* truelle *(f)* de briqueteur
Brillo ® pad *n* tampon *(m)* Jex ®
bristle *n* (single) poil *(m)*
bristles *npl* (on brush etc., real) soies *(fpl);*
(synth.) poils *(mpl)*
brittle *adj* (glass etc) cassant
broad *adj* (large) large
broken *adj* (glass; window) brisé; (object)
cassé

broken down *n* (machinery, vehicle) panne *(f);* (appliance, power tool) (not working) il / elle ne marche pas
bronze *n* (metal) bronze *(m)*
bronze *n/adj* (colour) couleur *(f)* de bronze
broom *n* balai *(m)*
brown *n/adj* (colour) marron *(m)*

Brush

brush *n* (gen.) brosse *(f)*

hand sweeping ~ : balayette *(f)*
broom : balai *(m)*
paint ~ : pinceau *(m)*
paperhanging ~ : brosse *(f)* de tapissier
chimney ~ : hérisson *(m)*

---

brush (to) *v* brosser
brushed *adj* (textiles) gratté
BTU *n* (British Thermal Unit) unité *(f)* calorifique
bucket *n* (general) seau *(m);* (of excavator, digger) godet *(m)*
budget *n* budget *(m)*

Builder

builder *n* (general) entrepreneur *(m)* en bâtiment

bricklayer *n* briqueteur *(m)*
builder (contractor, mason) maçon *(m);*
house ~ : entrepreneur *(m)* dans l'immobilier;
builder (employee) ouvrier (ière) dans le bâtiment
builder (firm) entreprise *(f)* de bâtiment

---

builder's yard *n* dépôt *(m)* de matériaux de construction
building *n* (house / flats / offices) immeuble *(m);* (general) bâtiment

building costs *npl* frais *(mpl)* de construction
building land *n* terrain *(m)* à bâtir
building materials *npl* matériaux *(mpl)* de construction
building permit *n* permis *(m)* de construire
building plot *n* terrain *(m)* à bâtir
building site *n* chantier *(m)* de construction
building society *n* société *(f)* de crédit immobilier
building surveyor *n* expert *(m)* géomètre
building work *n* ouvrage *(m)*
built-in *adj* (furniture) encastré
built-in washbasin *n* vasque *(f)*
bulb *n* (elec.) ampoule *(f)*; **(energy saving ~)** *n* ampoule *(f)* à faible consommation
bulb socket / holder *n* (elec.) douille *(f)*
(bayonet ~) douille *(f)* à baïonnette
(screw ~) douille *(f)* à vis
(wall mounted ~) plaque *(f)* d'applique
bulldozer *n* bulldozer *(m)*
bungalow *n* (gen.) pavillon *(m)*
bunghole *n* bonde *(f)*
bunk bed *n* (top) lit *(m)* du haut; (lower) lit *(m)* du bas
bunk beds *npl* lits *(mpl)* superposés
bureau *n* (office) bureau *(m)*; (office – gen. small) cabinet *(m)*; (branch office) agence *(f)*;
bureau *n* (writing desk) secrétaire *(m)*
burglar alarm *n* alarme *(f)* contre le vol
burglary *n* cambriolage *(m)*
burgle (to) *v* cambrioler
burner *n* (of cooker etc.) brûleur *(m)*
burnish *v* brunir
burnt sienna *n/adj* (colour) terre *(f)* de Sienne brûlée
burnt umber *n/adj* (colour) terre *(f)* d'ombre brûlée
burr walnut *n* (wood; branch) ronce *(f)* de noyer
burst (to) *v* (pipe; boiler) éclater
butane *n* butane *(m)*

butcher's hook *n*   crochet *(m)* en S
butt (to) *v*   abuter
butt joint *n*   joint *(m)* bout à bout
buzz saw *n*   scie *(f)* circulaire
buzzer *n*   sonnerie *(f)*

cabin *n* (hut) cabane *(f);* (holiday camp) chalet *(m)*

cabinet *n* (cupboard) petit placard *(m);* (display, drinks etc.) meuble *(m)* vitrine, bar; etc

cable *n* (gen.) câble *(m);* (domestic appliances) câble souple; (elec. installation) câble rigide; **(extension ~)** rallonge *(f)*

cable clip *n* serre câble *(m)*

cable cutter *n* coupe cable *(m)*

cable cutter / stripper *n* pince *(f)* à usages multiples

cable reel *n* enrouleur *(m)* de câble

cable stripper *n* pince *(f)* à dénuder

calico *n* calicot *(m)*

call-out charge *n* frais *(mpl)* de déplacement

callipers *npl* (measure) compas *(m)* d'épaisseur

Calor ® **gas bottle** *n* bouteille *(f)* du butane

camel hair *n* poil *(m)* de chameau

candle *n* bougie *(f)*

(church ~) cierge *(m)*

(household ~) bougie *(f)* de ménage

cane *n* (material) rotin *(m)*

cane furniture *n* mobilier *(m)* en rotin

canister *n* boîte *(f)* métallique

canton *n* canton *(m)*

canvas *n* (material) toile *(f)*

cap *n* (for screw head) cache *(m)* vis; (cover e.g. of valve) capuchon *(m);* (of bottle) capsule *(f)*

capacity *n* capacité *(f)*

capricorn beetle *n* capricorne *(m)*

carbide *n* carbure *(m)*

carbolic *adj* phéniqué

carbolic soap *n* savon *(m)* phéniqué

carbon *n* carbone *(m)*

carbon arc lamp *n* lampe *(f)* à arc

carbon monoxide *n* monoxyde *(m)* de carbone

Carborundum ® *n* carbure *(m)* de silicium; Carborundum ® *(m)*

cardboard *n* carton *(m)*

cardiac arrest *n* arrêt *(m)* du cour
carpenter *n* menuisier *(m)*; (heavy construction) charpentier *(m)*
carpenter's hammer *n* marteau *(m)* arrache clou; marteau *(m)* à panne fendue
carpenter's saw *n* scie *(f)* de charpentier
carpentry *n* (joiner, fitter) menuiserie *(f)*; (heavy onstruction) charpenterie *(f)*
carpet *n* (general) tapis *(m)*; (fitted) moquette *(f)*
(foam backed ~) avec un envers en mousse
carpet beetle *n* anthrène *(m)*
carpet fitter *n* poseur *(m)* de moquette
carpet sweeper *n* balai *(m)* mécanique
carpet tile *n* dalle *(f)* moquette
carrier *n* (transport co.) transporteur *(m)*
carrier (to send by ~) *v* expédier
carry (to) *v* porter
cart *n* **(hand ~)** charrette *(f)* (à bras)
cart (to) *v* trimballer
cartridge paper *n* papier *(m)* à dessin
carve (to) *v* (sculpt) tailler; sculpter.
case *n* (protective box) étui *(m)*; (small box) carton *(m)*; (large box, chest) caisse *(f)*
casement window *n* fenêtre *(f)* à battants
cash *n* espèces *(fpl)*; argent *(m)* liquide
cash (to pay in ~) *v* payer en espèces

Cash payments

Opportunities are always available to save money by employing people in the evening or at week-ends to do jobs 'Cash in Hand'. Doubtless you will make efforts to determine the probable quality of the work. In addition (particularly if you are not a full-time resident) it is as well to bear two factors in mind.

From time to time one may be exasperated with the nation's bureaucracy but it does at

---

Cash payments (continued)

least require that bone-fide building or
contracting enterprises are registered and that
they carry insurance to cover the cost of
making good any inferior work. It is also
possible (if not probable) that you may have
to pay the equivalent of Capital Gains Tax
whenever your property might be sold.
The rules are complex but one thing is certain
– you'll get no allowance for a couple of
hundred Euros passed across the table as
you enjoy a glass of local wine on a Sunday
evening!

Cash and carry   Cellar

cash and carry n   libre-service *(m) de* vent en
gros
cash desk n   caisse *(f)*
cash on delivery (COD) n   envoi *(m)* contre
remboursement
casing n (general) revêtement *(m)*
cask n (wine) tonneau *(m);* (beer) fût *(m)*
cast (to) v   (in metal) couler
cast iron n   fonte *(f)*
casting n   coulée *(f)*
castor n (furniture wheel) roulette *(f)*
castor oil n   huile *(f)* de ricin
catalogue n   catalogue *(m)*
cat flap n   chatière *(f)*
cavity block n   moellon *(m)* creux
cavity brick n   brique *(f)* creuse
cavity wall n   mur *(m)* creux
cavity wall insulation n   isolation *(f)* des
murs creux
ceiling n   plafond *(m)*
ceiling joist n   solive *(f)* de plafond
ceiling light n   plafonnier *(m)*
ceiling pull switch n   commutateur *(m)*
plafonnier à tirette
cellar n   cave *(f)*

Cement

cement *n* ciment *(m);*
dry mixed ~ : ciment *(m)* prêt à l'emploi;
quick setting ~ : ciment *(m)* prompt;
ready-to-mix *adj* (dry mix) prêt à gâcher
tile ~ : mastic *(m)*

---

cement (to) *v* cimenter
cement mixer *n* bétonnière *(f)*
centigrade *adj* Celsius
central heating *n* chauffage *(m)* central
centre bit *n* mèche *(f)* à bois
centre hung window *n* (vertical) fenêtre *(f)*
pivotante; (horizontal) fenêtre *(f)* basculante
ceramic *n* céramique *(f)*
ceramic *adj* en céramique
ceramic hob *n* table *(f)* de cuisson en
vitrocéramique
cesspit (cesspool) *n* fosse *(f)* d'aisances;
(septic tank) fosse *(f)* septique
chain *n* chaîne *(f)*
chain (to) *v* enchaîner
chainsaw *n* tronçonneuse *(f)*
chair *n* chaise *(f)*
chair *n* (upholstered) fauteuil *(m)*
chalet *n* (mountain) chalet *(m);* (holiday camp)
bungalow *(m)*
chalk *n* (powder) poudre *(f)* à tracer; (mineral)
craie *(f);* (for blackboard) bâton *(m)* de craie
chalkboard (blackboard) *n* tableau *(m)* noir
chamber *n* (room) chambre *(f)*
chamfer *n* chanfrein *(m)*
chamfer (to) *v* chanfreiner
chamois leather *n* peau *(f)* de chamois
chandelier *n* lustre *(m)*
charge *n* (price) prix *(m);* (cost of service)
frais *(m)*
(extra ~) supplément *(m)*
(no   extra ~) sans supplément *(m)*

charge (to) *v* (require payment) faire payer;
(battery) charger
charged *adj* (battery) chargé
check (to) *v* (verify) vérifier
checked *pp* vérifié
cherry *n* (wood, trees) cerisier *(m)*
cherry *n/adj* (colour) rouge cerise
chest *n* (furniture; luggage) coffre *(m);*
(container) caisse *(f)*
chest of drawers *n* commode *(f)*
chestnut *n* (timber) châtaignier *(m)*
(horse ~) *n* (tree) marronnier *(m)* (d'Inde)
(sweet ~) *n* (wood, trees) châtaignier *(m)*
cheval glass *n* psyché *(f)*
chime *n* (clock) carillon *(m)*
chimes *npl* (doorbell) carillon *(m)*
chimney *n* cheminée *(f)*
chimney breast *n* manteau *(m)* de cheminée
chimney cowl *n* capuchon *(m)* de cheminée
chimney flue *n* conduit *(m)* de cheminée
chimney pot *n* mitron *(m)* de cheminée
chimney sweep *n* ramoneur *(m)*
china *n* (fine crockery) porcelaine *(f)*
china cabinet / cupboard *n* placard *(m)* à
vaisselle
china clay *n* kaolin *(m)*
chipboard *n* aggloméré *(m)*
chippings *npl* gravillons *(mpl)*
chisel *n* ciseau *(m)*
(bricklayer's ~ / bolster) ciseau (x) *(m)* de
briqueteur
(wood ~) ciseau *(m)* à bois
chisel (to) *v* ciseler
chloride *n* chlorure *(m)*
chlorinate (to) *v* chlorer
chlorination *n* chloration
chlorine *n* chlore *(m)*
chop (to) *v* couper
chuck *n* (of power drill) mandrin *(m)*
cinder *n* (ash) cendre *(f)*
circuit *n* (elec.) circuit *(m)*

Circuit branch   Cobblestones

circuit branch *n* (elec.) branchement *(m)* de circuit

circuit breaker *n* (elec.) coupe circuit *(m);* disjoncteur *(m)*

circuit diagram *n* (elec.) schéma *(m)* de circuit

circuit tester *n* (elec.) testeur *(m)* de tension

circuitry *n* (elec.) ensemble *(m)* de circuit

circular saw *n* scie *(f)* circulaire

circulating pump *n* pompe *(f)* de circulation; circulateur *(m)* du chauffage central

cistern *n* (of WC) réservoir *(m)* du chasse d'eau; (in attic, underground) citerne *(f)*

cistern exit valve *n* (WC exit valve) clapet *(m)*

cladding *n* (general) revêtement *(m);* (panels) lambris *(m)*

clamp *n* (hold together) serre jointe *(f)*

clamp (to) *v* serrer

claw hammer *n* marteau *(m)* arrache clou; marteau *(m)* à panne fendue

clay *n* argile *(f)*

clean (to) *v* (of surfaces etc. during building & painting works) décaper

cleaning *n* (of surfaces etc. during building & painting works) décapage *(m)*

cleat *n* taquet *(m)*

clip *n* pince *(f)*

(crocodile ~) pince *(f)* crocodile

(jubilee ~) bague *(f)* de serrage

closet *n* (large walk in cupboard) penderie *(f)*

cloth *n* (duster, floor ~) chiffon *(m)*

clothes line *n* corde *(f)* à linge

(rotary ~) séchoir *(m)* parapluie

coach bolt / screw *n* tire-fond *(m)*

coach hook *n* (for shutter) crochet *(m)* de contrevent (pour volet)

coat *n* (of paint, plaster etc) couche *(f)*

coat (to) *v* (cover with) enduire

coating *n* (paint, plaster etc on surface) revêtement *(m)*

cobblestones *npl* pavés *(mpl)*

cobweb *n* toile *(f)* d'araignée
cockroach *n* cafard *(m)*
COD (c**ash on delivery**) *n* envoi *(m)* contre
remboursement
cold *n* froid *(m)*
collar *n* (on pipework) bague *(f)*
colour *n* couleur *(f)*
colours - (for a list of colours see "Paint and
Paintwork" on page
compression joint *n* (pipes with 'olive' seals)
raccord *(m)* à olive; raccord *(m)* instantané
concrete *n* béton *(m)*
(ready mix ~) béton *(m)* pré mélangé
concrete (to) *v* bétonner
concrete mixer *n* bétonnière *(f)*
conduit *n* (general) baguette *(f);* (pipe)
conduit *(m)*
connection *n* (elec.) branchement *(m);*
(pipework, elec.) raccordement *(m)*
connection box *n* (elec.) boîte *(f)* de
distribution; boîtier *(m)* de raccordement
connector *n* (elec. wire / cable) connecteur *(m)*

Connector (pipework)

connector *n* (pipework) raccord *(m); joint*
(m);

angle ~ : raccord courbe
elbow ~ : raccord coude
flexible connector ~ : (plumbing, lengthy)
flexible *(m)* d'alimentation
straight ~ : raccord droit
straight reducing ~ : raccord droit
(réduction)

---

conservatory *n* véranda *(f)*
construct (to) *v* construire
construction *n* construction *(f)*
construction industry *n* bâtiment *(m)*
constructor *n* constructeur (trice) *(m)/(f)*
consult (to) *v* consulter

consultant *n* consultant (e) *(m)/(f)*
consumer unit *n* (elec.) tableau *(m)* de répartition
consumer unit terminal *n* (elec.) borne *(f)* de raccordement
contaminated *adj* contaminé
contents *npl* (of property) biens *(mpl);* (of container, bag) contenu *(m)*
contort (to) *v* déformer
contour line *n* courbe *(f)* hypsométrique
contour map *n* carte *(f)* hypsométrique
contract *n* contrat *(m)* (for) pour; (with) avec.
contractor *n* entrepreneur (euse) *(m)/(f)*
control (to) *v* (direct) diriger

Conversion tables
See: Area (p. 5); Length (p. 52);
Volume (p. 102); Weight (p. 106).

---

convex *adj* convexe
cooker *n* cuisinière *(f)*
coping *n* chaperon *(m)*
coping saw *n* scie *(f)* à chantourner
coping stone *n* pierre *(f)* de chaperon
copper *n/adj* (metal, colour) cuivre *(m)*
copper beech *n* (tree) hêtre *(m)* pourpre
copper wire *n* fil *(m)* de cuivre
copperware *n* cuivres *(mpl)*
copra *n* copra(h) *(m)*
core *n* (of cable) âme *(f)*
cork *n* (material) liège *(m)*
cork *n* (bottle stopper) bouchon *(m)*
cork *n* (underlay) sous couche *(f)* liège
cork (to) *v* boucher
cork textured wallpaper *n* liège *(m)* sur papier peint
corner cupboard *n* encoignure *(f)*
corner stone *n* pierre *(f)* angulaire
cornice *n* corniche *(f)*
corridor *n* couloir *(m)*

Corrosion   Cross grained

corrosion *n* corrosion *(f)*
corrugated *adj* ondulé
corrugated iron *n* tôle *(f)* ondulée
cost *n* coût *(m);* prix *(m)*
cost price *n* prix *(m)* coûtant
cot *n* lit *(m)* de bébé
cottage *n* petite maison *(f)*
(country ~) maison *(f)* de campagne
cotter pin *n* goupille *(f)* fendue
cotton *n* coton *(m)*
cotton wool *n* ouate *(f)* (de coton)
couch *n* (sofa) canapé *(m)*
counter *n* (service desk) comptoir *(m)*
countersink (to) *v* (grind / drill hole) fraiser;
(embed screw / bolt in surface) noyer
country house *n* manoir *(m)*
courtyard *n* cour *(f)*
cover *n* (protective sheet) couverture *(f)*
cover (to) *v* (protect) couvrir
covering *n* (wall, floor) revêtement *(m)*
cowl *n* capuchon *(m)*
crack *n* (in wall, pottery etc) fêlure *(f); fissure *(f)*
cracked *adj* craquelé
cradle *n* (for baby) berceau *(f)*
craft *n* (artist etc.) art *(m)*
craftsman / woman *n* (artistic skills) artiste
(m)/(f); (manual skills) artisan (e) *(m)/(f)*
craftsmanship *n* dextérité *(f)*
crane *n* grue *(f)*
crate *n* (container) caisse *(f)*
create (to) *v* (business; trade) créer
creosote *n* créosote *(f)*
creosote (to) *v* créosoter
crimson *n/adj* (colour) cramoisi *(m)*
crockery *n* vaisselle *(f)*
crooked *adj* de travers
crosscut file *n* lime *(f)* à double taille
crosscut saw *n* scie *(f)* de travers
cross grained *adj* (wood) aux fibres
irrégulières

cross head screwdriver *n* tournevis *(m)* cruciforme
cross section *n* coupe *(f)* transversale
crowbar *n* pince monseigneur *(f)*
cupboard *n* placard *(m)*
cupboard (walk in ~) *n* penderie *(f)*
cup hook *n* crochet *(m)* à visser; (plastic coated) crochet à visser epoxy
cupola *n* coupole *(f)*
cup washer *n* rondelle *(f)* cuvette
current *n* courant *(m)*
curtain pole *n* tringle *(f)* à rideaux
curtain rail *n* rail *(m)* à rideaux
curtain rod *n* barre *(f)* à rideaux
cut (to) *v* couper
cutter *n* (sharp knife) couteau *(m)*

Cylinder

cylinder *n* (gen.) cylindre *(m)*

(hot water ~) ballon d'eau chaude;
(compressed air ~) cylindre à air comprimé
(electrically heated hot water ~) chauffe-eau *(m)* à électrique
(gas heated hot water ~) **chauffe-eau** *(m)* à gaz

---

cylinder lock *n* barillet *(m)*

Damage   Depot

damage *n* dégâts *(mpl)*
(fire ~) dégâts *(mpl)* du feu
damage (to) *v* **(cause ~ to….)** causer des
dégâts à ……
damp *n* humidité *(f)*
damp *adj* (building, wall floor etc.) humide
damp *n* **(rising ~)** humidité *(f)* s'élevant du
sol
damper *n* (in fireplace) registre *(m)*
damp proof *adj* imperméable
damp proof course *n* barrière *(f)*
d'étanchéité
damp proof membrane *n* couche *(f)* isolant
dark *adj* (room, paint etc.) sombre; foncé
darken (to) *v* foncer
DC *n* (elec. current) courant *(m)* continu
dead *adj* (elec. circuit) hors courant
dead bolt *n* (lock) verrou *(m)* à bouton
dead centre *n* point *(m)* mort
deadlock *n* verrou *(m)* haut sécurité;
verrou *(m)* à clé
deal *n* (timber) bois *(m)* blanc
death watch beetle *n* vrillette *(f)*
debris *n* décombres *(mpl)*
decay *n* (of building, façade) délabrement *(m);*
(rot) pourriture *(f)*
decorating works *n* travaux *(mpl)* de
décoration
decorator *n* décorateur (trice) *(m)/(f)*
decrepit *adj* (furniture) en mauvais état;
(building) délabré
deduct (to) *v* déduire
deep *adj* profond
deep end *n* grand bassin *(m)*
deepen (to) *v* (dig out) creuser
defect *n* défaut *(m)*
degrees centigrade *npl* degrés *(mpl)* Celsius
dehumidify (to) *v* déshumidifier
demolish (to) *v* démolir
demonstrate (to) *v* (illustrate) démontrer

demonstration *n* (of machines etc.)
démonstration *(f)*
department *n* (in a store) rayon *(m)*
depot *n* dépôt *(m)*
depth *n* profondeur *(f)*
derelict *adj* (ruined) en ruines
dereliction *n* abandon *(m)*
descale (to) *v* détartrer
descaler *n* détartrant *(m)*
design *n* conception *(f)*
(~ for …) plan *(m)* de …
(good ~) de conception bon
(poor ~) de conception mauvais
design (to) *v* concevoir
design specification *n* spécification *(f)* du
modèle
desk *n* (furniture) bureau *(m)*
(writing ~) secrétaire *(m)*
detached house *n* maison *(f)* individuelle
develop (to) *v* aménager
development *n* (of site) aménagement *(m)*;
(of housing) ensemble *(m)* d'habitation
diagnose (to) *v* (problem) identifier
diagonal *n* diagonale *(f)*
diagram *n* schéma *(m)*
dial *n* cadran *(m)*
dial (to) *v* (telephone a number) faire (un
numéro); composer (un numéro); ('call' a
person, place) appeler
diameter *n* diamètre *(m)*
(external ~) diamètre *(m)* externe
diamond *n* diamant *(m)*
diamond cutting disk *n* disque *(m)* diamant
diamond tile cutting disk *n* disque *(m)*
diamant carrelage
die cast *adj* moulé sous pression
die casting *n* moulage *(m)* sous pression
diesel *n* (car, van) diesel *(m)*
diesel engine *n* moteur *(m)* Diesel
diesel fuel; diesel oil *n* gazole *(m)*
dig (to) *v* creuser

digger *n* excavateur *(m);* pelleteuse *(f)*
digital *adj* numérique
dilute *adj* dilué
dilute (to) *v* diluer
dim *adj* (poorly lit) sombre
dim (to) *v* (fade) ternir
dimension *n* dimension *(f)*
dimmer switch *n* variateur *(m)* de lumière;
variateur *(m)* d'ambiance
dining room *n* salle *(f)* à manger
dining table *n* table *(f)* de salle à manger
direct current (DC) *n* (elec.) courant *(m)*
continu
dishwasher *n* lave vaisselle *(m)*
dispose (to) *v* (of furniture / things) disposer
dissolve (to) *v* (create solution) dissoudre
distil (to) *v* distiller
distillation *n* distillation *(f)*
distilled water *n* eau *(f)* distillée
ditch *n* fossé *(m)*
divan bed *n* divan-lit *(m)*
divider *n* (room) cloison *(f)*
dividers *npl* (drawing instrument) compas *(m)* à
pointes sèches
dividing *adj* (wall etc.) mitoyen (enne) *(m)/(f)*
dividing wall *n* mur *(m)* mitoyen
diviner *n* **(water ~)** sourcier (ière) *(m)/(f)*
divining rod *n* baguette *(f)* de sourcier
DIY (Do It Yourself) *n* bricolage *(m)*
dome *n* dôme *(m)*
door *n* porte *(f)*
(folding ~) porte *(f)* pliante
(sliding ~) porte *(f)* coulissante
door bell *n* sonnette *(m)*
door chain *n* chaînette *(f)* de sécurité
door chime *n* carillon *(m)* de porte
door closer *n* ferme-porte *(m)*
door frame *n* dormant *(m)*
door furniture *n* plaques *(fpl)* et poignées fpl
door handle *n* **poignée** *(f)*
door jamb *n* jambage *(m)*

Door knob   Drainage system

door knob *n* bouton *(m)* de porte
door knocker *n* heurtoir *(m)*; marteau *(m)* de porte
door latch *n* loquet *(m)* à poucier
door viewer (spyhole) *n* judas *inv*
doorstep *n* pas *(m)* de porte
doorstop *n* butoir *(m)*
doorway *n* (frame) embrasure *(f)* de porte
dormer window *n* lucarne *(f)*
double glazing *n* double vitrage *(m)*
double glaze (to ~) *v* mettre du double vitrage à ….
double lock *n* (high security) verrou *(m)* de sûreté
double lock (to) *v* fermer à double tour
dovetail *n* (joint) assemblage *(m)* à queue d'aronde
dowel *n* cheville *(f)*
dowel (to) *v* cheviller
down pipe *n* tuyau *(m)* de descente
downstairs *adj* (gen.) en bas; (ground floor) *n* rez-de-chaussée *(m)inv*
dowser *n* (water diviner) sourcier (ière) *(m)/(f)*
'dozer *n* bulldozer *(m)*
drain *n* (for escaping water) drain *(m)*; (sewer) égout *(m)*
drain (to) *v* (garden, standing water) drainer; (items after washing) égoutter
drain clearing fluid *n* déboucheur *(m)* liquide
drain plunger *n* (implement, gen.) déboucheur *(m)*; (rubber hemisphere) ventouse *(f)*
drain plunger pump *n* (hand pump to unblock drains) pompe *(f)* hydraulique à main pour déboucher
drain rods *npl* tiges *(fpl)* déboucher
(flexible ~) déboucheur *(m)* à tiges flexibles
drain tap *n* robinet *(m)* de vidange
drainage *n* drainage
drainage system *n* système *(m)* d'assainissement

draining board n égouttoir *(m)*
drainpipe n descente *(f)* de gouttière
draught n (cool air) courant *(m)* d'air
draught excluder n bourrelet *(m)*
draught proof *adj* calfeutré
draughtproof (to) v calfeutrer
draughtproofing n calfeutrage
drawer n (furniture) tiroir *(m)*
drawing pin n punaise *(f)*
drench (to) v (in paste, paint etc.) noyer
dresser n (sideboard) buffet *(m); (displaying
china)* vaisselier *(m)*

Drill

drill n (gen., DIY) perceuse *(f)*

hand twist ~ : chignole *(f)*
power ~ : perceuse électrique
hammer ~ : perceuse à percussion; marteau
perforateur
drill screwdriver n perceuse-visseuse *(f)*

---

drill (to) v (wood & substitutes) percer; (metal;
masonry) forer
drill bit n (wood) mèche *(f); (metal, masonry)*
foret *(m)*
drinking water n eau *(f)* potable
drip n goutte *(f)*
drip (to) v goutter
dry lining n cloison *(f)* sèche
dry rot n pourriture *(f)* sèche
dump (to) v déposer
dungarees n salopette *(f)*
dust n poussière *(f)*
dustbin n poubelle *(f)*
dust sheet n housse *(f)*
dustpan n pelle *(f)* à poussière
dwelling n logement *(m)*

Ear defenders   Elm

ear defenders *npl* casque *(m)* anti bruit
ear plugs *npl* boule *(f);* Quiès ® *(fpl)*
earth *n* (elec.) terre *(f)*
earth (to) *v* (elec.) mettre à terre
earth cable *n* (elec.) câble *(m)* de terre
earthed *adj* (elec.) au sol
earthing spike *n* (elec.) piquet *(m)* de terre
east *n* est *(m)*
east facing *adj* exposé à l'est
east side *n* du côté *(m)* est
eaves *npl* avant-toit *(m)*
ebony *n/adj* (timber) ébène *(f);* (tree)
ébénier *(m);* (colour) noir *(m)* d'ébène
effluent *n* effluent *(m)*
eggshell blue *n/adj* (colour) bleu *(m)* pâle
eggshell finish *n* (painting) peinture *(f)*
coquille d'œuf
electric *adj* électrique
electric cooker *n* cuisinière *(f)* électrique
electric meter *n* compteur *(m)* d'électricité
electric shock *n* décharge *(f)* électrique
electric shock *v* **(to get an ~)** prendre le
courant
electric socket *n* prise *(f)* électrique
electric wire *n* fil *(m)* électrique
electrician *n* électricien (ienne) *(m)/(f)*
electrician's screwdriver *n* tournevis *(m)*
d'électricien
electricity *n* électricité *(f)*
electricity meter *n* compteur *(m)* d'électricité
electricity supply *n* alimentation *(f)* en
électricité
electrocuted (to be ~) *v* (accident)
s'électrocuter
elevation *n* (architectural drawing) élévation *(f);*
(front ~) élévation de la façade
(side ~) élévation latérale / de profil
(rear ~) élévation d'arrière
elevator *n* (hoist) élévateur *(m)*
ellipse *n* ellipse *(f)*
elm *n* (wood) orme

emerald green *n/adj* (colour) vert *(m)*
émeraude
emergency *n* cas *(m)* d'urgence
emergency aid *n* secours *(m)* d'urgence

Emergency

**Europe wide emergency - ☎ 112
(Access to English speaking operators).
France Medical Assistance ☎ 15**
(Use a land-line telephone if possible so that
your call can be easily traced)
See also Medical Phrases and Body Part terms
inside back cover.

For other emergencies:
Police ☎ 17
Fire ☎ 18

---

emergency stop *n* arrêt *(m)* d'urgence
emergency stop button *n* bouton *(m)* d'arrêt
d'urgence
emery cloth *n* toile *(f)* émeri
employee *n* salarié (e) *(m)/(f)*
employer *n* employeur (euse) *(m)/(f)*
employment *n* travail *(m);* emploi *(m)*
employment (to seek ~) *v* chercher du
travail
employment agency *n* bureau *(m)* de
recrutement
empty *adj* vide
empty (to) *v* vider
emulsion paint *n* peinture *(f)* émulsion
enamel *n* émail; (kitchenware) en émail
enamel paint *n* peinture *(f)* laquée
engine *n* **(internal combustion ~)**
moteur *(m)*
engineer *n* (repair man) dépanneur *(m)*
enlarge (to) *v* agrandir

enterprise *n* (company) entreprise *(f)*
entrance *n* (point of entry) entrée *(f)*; (lobby)
vestibule *(m)*
entrepreneur *n* entrepreneur (euse) *(m)/(f)*
entry phone *n* interphone *(m)*
equip (to) *v* équiper
equipment *n* équipement *(m)*
equipped *adj* **(well ~)** bien équipé
escutcheon *n* cache~entrée *(m) inv*
establish (to) *v* (business, trade) créer
estate agency *n* agence *(f)* immobilière
estate agent *n* agent *(m)* immobilier
estimate *n* (written quote) devis *(m)*
estimate (to) *v* (guesstimate) évaluer
EU *n* **(European Union)** UE *(f)* (Union
(f) européenne)
examine (to) *v* examiner
example *n* exemple *(m)*
excavate (to) *v* creuser
excavator *n* tractopelle *(f)*; excavateur *(m)*
excluder strip *n* (draught; rain) bas *(m)* du
porte
expand (to) *v* (room, property) agrandir
expansion bolt *n* vis *(f)* à cheville expansible
expansion joint *n* joint *(m)* de dilatation
expenses *npl* frais *(mpl)*; 'Francis's' expenses
les frais *(mpl)* de 'Francis'
expert *n* spécialiste *(m)/(f)*; expert *(m)*
express *adv* **(to send by ~)** envoyer en
exprès
extension *n* (of property) agrandissement
extension cable *n* rallonge *(f)*
extension ladder *n* échelle *(f)* coulissante
exterminate (to) *v* (vermin) éliminer
extinguish (to) *v* (fire) éteindre
extinguisher *n* extincteur *(m)*
extra charge *n* supplément *(m)*
(no ~) sans supplément
extractor fan *n* ventilateur *(m)* d'extraction
eyelet *n* œillet *(m)*

fabric *n*   tissu *(m)*
fabric textured wallpaper *n*   tissu *(m)* sur papier peint
façade *n*   façade *(f)*
fact sheet *n*   bulletin *(m)* d'informations
factory *n*   usine *(f)*
fade (to) *v* (loose intensity)   faner
faded *adj*   décoloré
fan *n* (for cooling)   ventilateur *(m)*
farmhouse *n*   ferme *(f)*
(small ~) *n* (gen. ancient)   fermette *(f)*
fault *n* (elec.)   défaut *(m)*
fax *n*   fax *(m);* télécopie *(f)*
fax (to) *v*   faxer; télécopier
fax machine *n*   télécopieur *(m)*
fax number *n*   numéro *(m)* de fax / télécopie
feather duster *n*   plumeau *(m)*
feeler gauge *n*   calibre *(m)* d'épaisseur
felt *n* (roofing)   carton *(m)* bitumé
fence *n* (boundary)   clôture *(f)*
fence post *n*   poteau (x) *(m)* de clôture
fence post holder / sole plate *n* (metal)   semelle *(f)*
(metal, bolt fixed ~)   semelle *(f)* boulonnée;
(with metal stake ~)   semelle *(f)* sur piquet métallique
fencing *n*   clôtures *(fpl)*
ferro concrete *n*   béton *(m)* armé
ferrous *adj*   ferreux (euse)
fibre *n* (textiles, wood)   fibre *(f)*
(artificial ~)   fibre *(f)* artificielle
(synthetic ~)   fibre *(f)* synthétique
fibreboard *n*   panneau *(m)* en aggloméré
fibreglass *n*   fibres *(fpl)* de verre
filament *n* (elec.)   filament *(m)*

File

file *n* (tool) lime *(f);*
flat ~ : lime plate;
half round ~ : lime mi ronde;
triangular ~ : lime tiers-point;
mini ~ : lime de précision

---

file (to) *v* (metal, timber) limer
filing cabinet *n* classeur *(m)* à tiroirs
fill (to) *v* (crack, hole) reboucher; (ditch, hollow) remblayer
filler *n* (product) enduit *(m);* reboucheur *(m);* (quick setting) enduit *(m)* à prise rapide
final invoice *n* facture *(f)* définitive
fine tooth saw *n* scie *(f)* à denture américaine
fine grained *adj* (timber) au grain fin
finger plate *n* plaque *(f)* de propreté
finial *n* fleuron *(m)*
finish *n* (quality of appearance) finition *(f)*
fir *n* (wood, tree) sapin *(m)*
fire *n* (gen.) feu *(m);* (major) incendie *(m)*
fire alarm *n* alarme *(f)* contre le feu; alarme *(f)* incendie
fire blanket *n* couverture *(f)* anti feu
fire brick *n* brique *(f)* réfractaire
fire damage *n* dégâts *(mpl)* du feu
fire door *n* porte *(f)* coupe feu
fire escape *n* escalier *(m)* de secours
fire exit *n* sortie *(f)* de secours
fire extinguisher *n* extincteur *(m)*
fire hazard *n* risque *(m)* d'incendie
fire hydrant *n* bouche *(f)* d'incendie
fire regulations *npl* normes *(f)* de protection contre les incendies
fire screen *n* écran *(m)* de cheminée
fire service *n* sapeurs-pompiers *(mpl)*
firelighter *n* allume feu *(m)*
fireplace *n* cheminée *(f)*

Fireproof   Flatpack

fireproof *adj* ignifugé
fireproof (to) *v* ignifuger
fireproofed plasterboard *n* plaque *(f)* de plâtre ignifugée
firewall *n* mur *(m)* coupe feu
firewood *n* bois *(m)* à brûler
firm *n* (business) entreprise *(f)*
firm *adj* (solid) solide
first aid *n* premiers soins *(mpl)*
first class *adj* première classe (de)
first floor *n* premier étage *(m)*
fishpond *n* (in garden) bassin *(m)*
fissure *n* (in building) fissure *(f)*
fit (to) *v* (item in place) mettre *(item)* en place
fitted *adj* (cupboards, kitchens) intégré
fitted carpet *n* moquette *(f)*
fitter *n* (white goods) monteur (euse) *(m)/(f);*
(carpet ~) poseur *(m)* de moquette
(gas ~) chauffagiste *(m)*
fix (to) *v* (position) poser; (put in place) fixer
fixed *adj; pp* fixé;
fixings *npl* (screws and bolts) visserie *(f)*
fixture *n* (immovable thing) installation *(f)*
fixtures and fittings *n* (property deals) équipements *(mpl)*
flagpole *n* mât *(m)*
flagstone *n* dalle *(f)*
flake off (to) *v* (paint etc.) s'écailler; (plaster, cladding etc.) s'effriter
flame *n* flamme *(f)*
flame retardant *n* ignifugeant *(m)*
flame coloured *adj* (colour) rouge feu *inv*
flamethrower *n* lance flammes *(m)inv*
flammable *adj* inflammable
(highly ~) hautement inflammable
flange *n* collet *(m)*
flap *n* (in surface, on table) abattant *(m)*
flashlight / torch *n* lampe *(f)* de poche
flat *n* (dwelling) appartement *(m)*
flat *adj* (horizontal) plat
flat pack *adj* en kit

flex *n* (elec.) câble *(m)* souple
flexible connector *n* (plumbing, lengthy)
flexible *(m)* d'alimentation

Flexible connectors

Flexibles or more fully *flexibles d'alimentation* have long been a part of the kit used by French plumbers (or at least the DIYers of that ilk). They are similar to the metal-armoured hydraulic pipes found in cars, tractors and lifting machinery.

For the *maison* they are available in a variety of lengths and in diameters corresponding to the supply pipes of kitchen and bathroom fittings. The ends are fitted with a wide choice of appropriate connectors. While individually comparatively expensive they may save hours of work constructing tubular sculptures in awkward corners and spaces!

---

float *n* **(plasterer's ~)** (tool) taloche *(f)*
(steel ~) platoir *(m)* à enduire inoxydable
(wooden ~) taloche *(f)* bois
float (for tamping tiles) batte *(f)*
float *n* (for float valve) flotteur *(m)*
float arm *n* (for float valve) bras *(m)inv* de flotteur
float valve *n* (WC) robinet *(m)* à flotteur
flock wallpaper *n* papier peint *(m)* floqué
flood (to) *v* (house, area) inonder
flood / flooding *n* inondation *(f)*
floor *n* (gen. / stone) sol *(m);* (storey) étage *(m);* (planking) plancher *(m);* (wood block) parquet *(m)*
floor area *n* superficie *(f)*
floor covering *n* (not carpet) revêtement *(m)* de sol
floor plan *n* plan *(m)*

floor board *n* (composite) latte *(f)*; (planks)
plancher *(fpl)*
flower bed *n*   parterre *(m)* de fleurs
flower garden *n*   jardin *(m)* d'agrément
flue *n* (in general = chimney) cheminée *(f)*;
(of stove, boiler) tuyau *(m)*
flue gas *n*   gaz *(m)* de haut fourneau
flue liner *n*   conduit *(m)*
fluorescent tube *n*   tube *(m)* fluorescente
fluorescent tube holder *n*   réglette *(f)*
fluorescente
flux *n*   décapant *(m)*
fly *n* (insect) mouche *(f)*
foam insulation *n*   isolation *(f)* thermique en
mousse
folding door *n*   porte *(f)* pliante
foreman, forewoman *n*   maître (esse) *(m)/(f)*
d'œuvre; chef *(m)* d'atelier
fork *n* (garden tool) fourche *(f)*; bêche *(f)* à
dents
Formica ® *n*   formica ® *(m)*
formwork *n*   coffrage *(m)*
foundations *npl*   fondations *(fpl)*
foundry *n*   fonderie *(f)*
four stroke *adj* (engine) quatre temps
frame *n* (of door) dormant *(m)*; (window, picture)
cadre *(m)*
frame saw *n*   scie *(f)* à monture de menuisier
frame house *n*   maison *(f)* à charpente en
bois
framework *n* (metal) ossature *(f)*; (timber)
charpente *(f)*
French chalk *n*   craie *(f)* de tailleur
French doors *n*   porte fenêtre *(f)*
French window *n*   porte fenêtre *(f)*
fretsaw *n*   scie *(f)* à découper
fretwork *n*   découpure *(f)*
frieze *n*   frise *(f)*
frontage *n* (of house) façade *(f)*
fuel *n* (vehicles, machines) carburant *(m)*
fuel oil *n*   fioul *(m)*

fuel tank *n* resevoir *(m)* de fioul
full *adj* plein
fungal *adj* fongique
fungal infection *n* mycose *(f)* fongique
funnel *n* (for pouring) entonnoir *(m)*
furnace *n* (central heating boiler) chaudière *(f)*
furniture *n* meubles *(mpl);* mobilier *(m)*
furniture beetle *n* vrillette *(f)*
furniture remover *n* déménageur *(m)*
furniture store *n* (shop) magasin *(m)* de
meubles
fuse *n* (elec.) fusible *(m);* plomb *(m)*
fuse (a ~ has blown) un fusible a sauté
fuse (cartridge) *n* fusible *(m)* à cartouche
fuse (to) *v* (to blow the fuses) faire sauter les
plombs
fuse box *n* boite *(f)* à fusibles
fuse board *n* tableau *(m)* de fusibles

galvanised nail *n* pointe *(f)* galvanisée
galvanize (to) *v* galvaniser
garden *n* jardin *(m)*
garden shears *npl* cisailles *(fpl)* de jardinier
garden suburb *n* banlieue *(f)* vert
garden waste *n* déchets *(mpl)* de jardin
gardener *n* jardinier (ière) *(m)/(f)*
gardening *n* jardinage *(m)*
gas *n* gaz *(m)*
gas (to) *v* gazer
gas bottle *n* (small; for blowlamp etc.)
cartouche *(f)* de gaz
gas connector *n* (for appliances using bottle
gas) raccord *(m)* de gaz
gas cooker *n* cuisinière *(f)* à gaz
gas cylinder *n* (Calor ® type) bouteille *(f)* de
gaz
gas fire *n* appareil *(m)* de chauffage à gaz
gas fitter *n* chauffagiste *(m)*
gas heater *n* (for water) chauffe-eau *(m)* à gaz
gas lamp / gaslight *n* lampe *(f)* à gaz
gas main *n* canalisation *(f)* de gaz
gas meter *n* compteur *m)* à gaz
gas oven *n* four *(m)* à gaz
gas range *n* fourneau *(m)* à gaz
gas ring *n* (fixed) brûleur *(m)* à gaz; (portable)
réchaud *(m)* à gaz
gas stove *n* cuisinière *(f)* à gaz
gas tap *n* robinet *(m)* de gaz
gate *n* (house and garden) porte *(f)*; (more
elaborate) portail *(m)*; (of field) barrière *(f)*
gate control *n* **(remote ~)** motorisation *(f)* de
porte / portail
gate latch *n* platine *(f)* pivotante
gate valve *n* vanne *(f)*
gatepost *n* poteau *(m)* d'angle
gauge *n* (gen. term) appareil *(m)* de mesure
gazebo *n* belvédère *(m)*
gemstone *n* pierre *(f)* brute
generator *n* (elec.) générateur *(m)*
gimlet *n* tartière *(f)*

glass *n* (gen.) verre *(m)*
glass cloth *n* essuie verres *(m)*

Glass cutting

As with timber (page 81) most larger DIY stores provide an on-the-spot glass cutting service. Typically they will have a container of small samples of standard, frosted and ornamental glass in various qualities for examination. Make your choice, give the size required and the operator will provide! The material will be priced according to its area.

---

glass cutter *n* (tool) coupe verre *(f);* diamant *(m)*
(circular ~) compas *(m)* de coupe verre
glass fibre *n* fibre *(f)* de verre
glass paper *n* papier *(m)* de verre
glass wool *n* laine *(f)* de verre
glaze (to) *v* (window etc) vitrer
glazed *adj* (window etc) vitré
glazier *n* vitrier *(m)*
gloss coat *n* (of paint) couche *(f)* de peinture brillante
gloss paint *n* peinture *(f)* brillante
glue *n* colle *(f)*
glue for..... colle pour....
glue (to) *v* coller
glue pen *n* stylo *(m)* colle
glue stick *n* bâton *(m)* de colle
gradient *n* pente *(f)*
grain *n* (in wood) grain *(m)* de veines
granary *n* grenier *(m)*
granite *n* granit(e) *(m)*
grass *n* (general) herbe *(f);* (= lawn) pelouse *(f)*
grassed area *n* (also turf) gazon *(m)*
grate *n* (fire container) grille *(f)* de foyer
grate *n* (hearth) âtre *(m)*
grating *n* grille *(f)*

gravel *n* (coarse) graviers *(mpl)*: *(*fine)
gravillons *(mpl)*
gravel (to) *v* gravillonner
gravel pit *n* gravière *(f)*
gravelled *adj* (drive; path; area) gravillonné
grazing *n* pacage *(m)*
grazing land *n* pâturage *(m)*
grazing rights *npl* droit *(m)* de pacage
grease *n* (= lubricant) graisse *(f)*
grease (to) *v* graisser
grease gun *n* pompe *(f)* à graisse
green field site *n* terrain *(m)* vierge
greenhouse *n* serre *(f)*
grey *n/adj* (colour) gris *(m)*
grind (to) *v* affûter
grinder *n* (occupation, knife sharpener) affûteur
(m); rémouleur (euse) *(m)/(f)*
grinding *n* affûtage *(m)*
grinding disk *n* meule *(f)*
grindstone *n* (millstone / grindstone) meule *(f)*
(sharpening stone) pierre *(f)* à aiguiser
groove *n* (carpentry, masonry) rainure *(f)*
groove *n* (in screw) fente *(f);* creux *(m)*
grooved *adj* rainé
ground *n* (floor) sol *(m);* (land) terre *(f);*
(area) terrain *(m)*
(above ~) en surface *(f)*
(below ~) sous terre *(f)*
ground floor *n* rez-de-chaussée *(m)inv*
ground level (access etc.) niveau *(m)* du sol
grounds *npl* (of private property) parc *(m)*
grouting *n* masticage *(m)*
growth area *n* secteur *(m)* en expansion
grub screw *n* vis *(f)* sans tête
gully *n* (rainwater, dishwater) caniveau *(m)*
gutter *n* (on eaves) gouttière *(f);* (ground
level) caniveau *(m)*
guttering *n* gouttières *(fpl)*
gypsum *n* gypse *(m)*

Habitable   Hard hat

habitable *adj* habitable
hack (to) *v* (strike at) taillader
hack off (to) *v* tailler
hacksaw *n* scie *(f)* à métaux
half *n* (one of two equal parts) **moitié** *(f)*
half *adj* (1/2 = a measure) demi
half-timbered *n* colombages *m*
half-timbered house *n* maison *(f)* normande;
maison *(f)* à colombage
hall *n* (in house) entré *(f)*
halogen lamp *n* lampe *(f)* halogène

Hammer

hammer *n* marteau *(m)*

carpenter's / claw hammer *n* marteau *(m)*
arrache clou; marteau *(m)* à panne fendue
club / lump hammer *n* massette *(f)*;
marteau *(m)* de maçon
sledge hammer *n* masse *(f)*
tack hammer *n* marteau *(m)* de tapissier

---

hammer (to) *v* (to beat) marteler
hammer beam *n* blochet *(m)*
hammer drill *n* perceuse *(f)* à percussion;
marteau *(m)* perforateur
hand *adj* **(by ~)** à la main
hand basin *n* lavabo *(m)*
hand painted *adj* peint à la main
hand saw *n* scie *(f)* égoïne; scie *(f)* manuelle
hand twist drill *n* chignole *(f)*
handcart *n* charrette *(f)* à bras
handle *n* (of door, furniture) poignée *(f)*;
(of tools, cutlery) manche *(m)*
handle (to) *v* (manipulate) manipuler; (deal
with) traiter
handrail *n* (also 'banister') rampe *(f)*
handyman *n* bricoleur *(m)*
hard (brazing) solder *n* brasure *(f)*
hard hat *n* (safety helmet) casque *(m)*

hard water *n* eau *(f)* calcaire
hardboard *n* isorel *(m)*
hardware dealer *n* quincaillier (ère) *(m)/(f)*
hardware shop *n* quincaillerie *(f)*
hardwood *n* bois *(m)* dur
hatch *n* (gen. access) trappe *(f)* d'access;
(service ~) passe plats *(m)*
hatchet *n* hachette *(f)*
haulage *n* transport *(m)* routier
haulage charge *n* frais *(mpl)* de transport
haulier *n* transporteur *(m)*
hawk *n* (trowel with handle underneath)
taloche *(f)*
H-beam *n* poutrelle *(f)* en 'H'
heart *n* cœur *(m)*
heart attack *n* crise *(f)* cardiaque
heart trouble *n* problèmes *(mpl)* cardiaques
hearth *n* (hearthstone) âtre *(m);* (more figurative;
≈ home) foyer *(m)*
heat *n* chaleur *(f)*
heat proof *adj* résistant à la chaleur
heat pump *n* thermopompe *(f);* pompe *(f)* à
chaleur
heat treated *adj* traité thermiquement
heater *n* (mobile) chauffage *(m)* d'appoint
heating *n* chauffage *(m)*
(central ~) *n* chauffage *(m)* central;
(underfloor ~) chauffage *(m)* par le sol
heating engineer *n* chauffagiste *(m)*
heating oil *n* fioul *(m);* mazout *(m)*
heating system *n* système *(m)* de chauffage
heavy *adj* lourd
heavy duty *adj* à haute résistance
hectare *n* (area) 10,000 sq m (= 2.47 acres)
hedge *n* haie *(f)*
hedge clippers *npl* cisailles *(fpl)* à haies
hedge trimmer *n* (power) taille-haies *(m)inv*
height *n* (of object) hauteur *(f)*
help *n* (assistance) aide *(f)*
help *n* (in emergency) secours *(m)* d'urgence
helpdesk *n* service *(m)* d'assistance

helpline *n* service *(m)* d'assistance téléphonique
hemp *n* (fibre) chanvre *(m)*
hemp rope *n* corde *(f)* de chanvre
hessian *n* toile *(f)* de jute
high pressure washer *n* nettoyeur *(m)* haute pression
high tension *adj* à haute tension
high voltage *n* haute tension
Highways Department *n* Service *(m)* des Ponts et Chaussées
hinge *n* (gen.) charnière *(f)*
(lift-off ~) gond *(m); paumelle *(f)*
(lifting ~) paumelle *(f)* à rampe
(strap ~) penture *(f)*
hinged *adj* (top) à charnières; (seat) rabattable; (component) articulé
hire *n* (machinery, vehicles, property) location *(f)*
hire (for ~) *n* (sign) à louer
hire company *n* agence *(f)* de location
historic building *n* monument *(m)* historique
hit *n* (strike a blow) coup *(m)*
hit (to) *v* (strike) frapper
hob *n* (elec. stove) table *(f)* de cuisson;
(ceramic ~) table *(f)* de cuisson en vitrocéramique
hoe *n* binette *(f); houe *(f)*
hoe (to) *v* (ground) biner; (plants; flowerbed) sarcler
hoist *n* palan *(m)*
hoist (to) *v* hisser
holding *n* (land) exploitation *(f)*
hole *n* (in timber, clothing) trou *(m);* (in wall) brèche *(f)*
hole saw *n* scie *(f)* clocher
holly *n* (wood; tree) houx *(m)*
home *n* logement *(m)*
home owner *n* propriétaire *(m)/(f)*
homestead *n* (smallholding) petite exploitation *(f)* agricole
hone (to) *v* (make sharp) aiguiser

honing stone *n*   pierre *(f)* à aiguiser

Hook

hook *n* (gen., wall fixture) crochet *(m);*

butcher's ~ : crochet en S;
coach ~ (for shutter) **:** crochet de contrevent (pour volet)
cup /screw ~ : crochet à visser; (plastic coated black / white); crochet à visser epoxy noir / blanc
right angled screw ~ : **gond** *(m)* à visser

---

hook *n* (horticultural) faucille *(f)*
hook (to) *v* (attach) accrocher
horse chestnut *n* (tree) marronnier *(m)* (d'Inde)
hose clip *n*   collier *(m)*
hosepipe *n*   tuyau *(m)* d'arrosage
hot *adj*   chaud
hothouse *n* (greenhouse) serre *(f)* chaude
hot water cylinder / heater *n* chauffe-eau *(m)*
house *n* maison *(f)*

House – and housing

For a list of various 'house' designations – see next page

---

house agent *n*   agent *(m)* immobilier
house in the country *n*   maison *(f)* de campagne
housing development *n* (small) lotissement *(m)*
housing estate *n* (large) cité *(f)*
humid *adj*   humide
humidifier *n*   humidificateur *(m)*
humidity *n*   humidité *(f)*

House – and housing

house *n* maison *(f)*
bungalow *n* pavillon *(m)*
cottage *n* petite maison *(f)*
country house *n* manoir *(m)*
detached house *n* maison *(f)* individuelle
family home *n* maison *(f)* familiale
farm house *n* ferme *(f);* (small, gen. ancient) fermette *(f)*
flat *n* (dwelling) appartement *(m)*
half timbered house *n* maison *(f)* à colombage; maison *(f)* normande
home *n* logement *(m)*
homestead *n* (smallholding) petite exploitation
house in the country *n* maison *(f)* de campagne
luxury home *n* maison *(f)* de standing
manor *n* manoir *(m)*
manor house *n* maison *(f)* de maître
manse *n* presbytère *(m)*
mansion *n* demeure *(f);* maison *(f)* bourgeoise
semi-detached house *n* maison *(f)* jumelée
show flat *n* appartement *(m)* témoin
show house *n* maison *(f)* témoin
small house maisonnette *(f)*
terrace *n* alignement *(m)* de maisons
thatched cottage *n* chaumière *(f)*
town house maison *(f)* de ville
villa *n* (large town house) pavillon *(m);* (holiday home) villa *(f)*

Hurt   Hydrant

hurt (to) *v* faire mal
hurt (to ~ oneself) *v* se blesser
hydrant *n* prise *(f)* d'eau
(fire ~) bouche *(f)* d'incendie

immersion heater n (electrically heated cylinder) chauffe eau *(m)* électrique
imperial measure adj conforme aux normes britanniques
impermeable adj (membrane, rock) imperméable
implement n (tool) outil *(m)*
inch n (measure) pouce *(m)* = 2.54cm
indestructible adj indestructible
inflammable adj inflammable
infrared sensor n détecteur *(m)* infrarouge
injure (to) v blesser
injured adj blessé
(seriously ~) grièvement blessé
inlet n (valve etc.) entrée *(f)*
inlet pipe n tuyau *(m)* d'entrée
instruction book n livret *(m)* de l'utilisateur
instructions npl instructions *(fpl)*
instrument n instrument *(m)*
insulate v (general) isoler; (against noise) insonoriser; (against heat / cold) calorifuger
insulating material n isolant *(m)*
insulation n **(thermal ~)** isolation *(fpl);* (of water tank) calorifugeage *(m);* (against noise) insonorisation *(f)*
insulator n (elec.) isolateur *(m)*
insurance n (gen.) assurance *(f)*
insure (to) v faire assurer
insured adj assuré
insurer n assureur *(m)*
intercom n interphone *(m)*
invention n invention *(f)*
inventor n inventeur (trice) *(m)/(f)*
inverted adj (upside down) à la envers
inverter n (elec.) onduleur *(m)*
investigate (to) v (have a look at) examiner; (enquire about) enquêter sur…
investigator n (fraud, insurance) enquêteur (trice) *(m)/(f)*

Invoices
The tills at French DIY stores are fitted with two print-out options. They can issue either a standard till receipt or a full itemised invoice. If you wish your purchase to be accepted in ANY 'official' circumstance – whether taxation, accountancy, legal or any other – you must ask for an invoice (you need only ask *"Facture , si'l vous plait"*). Such demands are routine and will cause no consternation. They must also be made out to you at your address. It can often be helpful to have these details to hand on a letter-heading or visiting card for the check-out operator to copy.

---

invoice *n* facture *(f)*
(final ~) facture *(f)* définitive
invoice *v* **(to send an ~ to…)** envoyer une facture à …
invoice *v* **(to receive an ~)** recevoir une facture
involve (to) *v* (cause participation) faire participer
iodine *n* (antiseptic) teinture *(f)* d'iode
iron *n* fer *(m)*
(scrap ~) ferraille *(f)*
(smoothing ~) fer *(m)* à repasser
iron craftsman / woman *n*
ferronnier (ière) *(m)/(f)*
iron fittings *npl* ferrure *(f)*
iron work *n* ferronnerie *(f)*
ironing *n* repassage *(m)*
ironing board *n* planche *(f)* à repasser
ironmonger *n* quincaillier (ère) *(m)/(f)*
ironmongery *n* quincaillerie *(f)*
isolate *v* isoler
isolated *adj* isolé
isolation *n* isolement *(m)*
ivory *n* (material) ivoire *(m)*
ivory *n/adj* (colour) ivoire *(m)*

jack *n* (for lifting weights) cric *(m)*
jack plug *n* jack *(m)*
jack knife *n* couteau *(m)* pliant
Jacuzzi ® *n* jacuzzi ® *(m)*; bain *(m)* bouillonnant
jade *n* (stone) jade *(m)*; *adj* (colour) vert jade *inv*
jam *n* (of machine) blocage *(m)*; (traffic) embouteillage *(m)*
jamb *n* (door) jambage *(m)*; (wedge etc. to stabilise) jambage *(m)*
japan *n* (lacquer) laque *(f)*
japan (to) *v* laquer; vernir
jaws *npl* (of tool) mâchoires *(fpl)*
JCB ® *n* (excavator) tractopelle *(f)*; JCB ® *(m)*
jemmy *n* (lever) pince monseigneur *(f)*
jemmy (to) *v* (lever) forcer (à la pince monseigneur)
jerry built *adj* construit à la va vite
jerrycan *n* jerrican *(m)*; nourrice *(f)*
jigsaw *n* scie *(f)* sauteuse
job *n* (available work) travail *(m)*; (task) tâche *(f)*; (occupation) métier *(m)*
jobber *n* travailleur (euse) *(m)/(f)* à la tâche
jobbing *adj* à la tâche
join *n* raccord *(m)*
join (to) *v* (fix together) joindre; réunir
joiner *n* menuisier (ière) *(m)/(f)*
joinery *n* menuiserie *(f)*

Joint

joint *n* (gen.) joint *(m)*

metalwork ~ : joint *(m)*
pipework ~ : raccord *(m)*
woodwork ~ : assemblage *(m)*
capillary (soldered) pipe ~ : raccord *(m)* cuivre à souder;
copper pipe ~ : raccord *(m)* cuivre;
compression ~ : (for metal pipes) raccord *(m)* à olive

Joint sealing tape   Jute

joint sealing tape *n* (PTFE) ruban *(m)*
Téflon ® d'étanchéité
joist *n* solive *(f)*
jubilee clip *n* bague *(f)* de serrage
junction box *n* (elec.) boîte *(f)* de
raccordement
junk room *n* débarras *(m)*
jute *n* jute *(m)*

Kerb   Knife sharpener

kerb *n* bord *(m)* du trottoir
kerbstone *n* pierre *(f)* de bordure d'un trottoir
kerosene *n* (paraffin) pétrole *(m)*
key *n* (for lock) clé *(f)*; (for radiator) clavette *(f)* à
radiateur
key card *n* carte *(f)* magnétique
keyhole *n* trou *(m)* de serrure
keyhole saw *n* scie *(f)* à guichet
key ring *n* porte clés *(m)*
keys *n* **(a bunch of ~)** un jeu *(m)* de clés
keystone *n* clé *(f)* de voûte
kiln *n* four *(m)*
kiss of life *n* bouche-à-bouche *(m)*
kit *n* (for self assembly) kit *(m)*
kitchen *n* cuisine *(f)*
(back ~) arrière cuisine
kitchen area *n* coin *(m)* cuisine
kitchen cabinet *n* (furniture) buffet *(m)* de
cuisine
kitchen range *n* fourneau *(m)* (de cuisine)
kitchen sink *n* évier *(m)*
kitchen unit *n* élément *(m)* de cuisine
knee pad *n* genouillère *(f)*
knife *n* couteau *(m)*
knife sharpener *n* (device) aiguisoir *(m)*
knife sharpener *n* (occupation) aiguiseur *(m)*;
affûteur *(m)*; rémouleur (euse) *(m)/(f)*

knob *n* (on furniture, decorative) boule *(f):*
(door ~) bouton *(m)*
knot *n* (in wood, string) nœud *(m)*
knocker *n* **(door ~)** heurtoir *(m)*
knock down (to) *v* (building, property) abattre

labour relations *npl* relations *(fpl)* du travail
labourer *n* (gen. worker / hard worker)
travailleur (euse) *(m)/(f);* (unskilled worker)
manœuvre *(m)*
(manual ~) ouvrier (ière) *(m)/(f):* (often linked
to trade e.g. : ~ maçon *building worker;* ~
menuisier *carpenter)*
lacquer *n* laque *(f)*
lacquer (to) *v* laquer
lacquer ware *n* laques *(mpl)*
lacquered *adj* laqué

Ladder

ladder *n* échelle *(f)*

extending ~ : échelle *(f)* télescopique
loft ~ : (gen.) échelle *(f)* d'accès;
loft ~ : (collapsible) échelle *(f)* accordéon;
loft ~ : (retractable) échelle *(f)* escamotable;
loft ~ : (sliding) echelle *(f)* coulissante
step ~ : escabeau (x) *(m)*

---

ladder stay *n* (adjustable / extending feet)
béquille *(f)*
lag (to) *v* (in plumbing) calorifuger; (in roof)
isoler
lagging *n* calorifugeage *(m);* isolant *(m)*
lagging jacket *n* garniture *(f)* de chauffe-eau
lake *n* lac *(m);* (smaller, pond) étang *(m)*
lakeside *n* **(by the ~)** au bord du lac

Laminate   Lath

laminate *n* (plastic) stratifié *(f);* (metal)
laminé *(m)*
laminated *adj* (plastic) stratifié; (metal) laminé;
(wood, ply) contreplaqué; (card) plastifié
lamp *n* lampe *(f)*
lamp holder *n* douille *(f)*
lampshade *n* abat-jour *(m)*
land agent *n* expert *(m)* foncier
land owner *n* propriétaire *(m)/(f)*
land registry *n* cadastre *(m)*
landfill site *n* site *(m)* d'enfouissement des
déchets
landing *n* (staircase) palier *(m)*
land line *n* (phone) ligne *(f)* de terre
landlord / landlady *n* (property
owner) propriétaire *(m)/(f)*
landscape *n* paysage *(m)*
landscape architect *n* architecte *(m)/(f)*
paysagiste
landscape gardener *n* jardinier (ière)
(m)/(f) paysagiste
landscape gardening *n* paysagisme *(m)*
landslide / landslip *n* glissement *(m)* de
terrain
lane *n* (rural) chemin *(m);* (minor road) petite
route *(f);* (in town) ruelle *(f)*
lantern *n* lanterne *(f)*
lap joint *n* joint *(m)* à recouvrement
lap riveting *n* rivetage *(m)* par recouvrement
lap welding *n* soudure *(f)* à recouvrement
larch *n* (wood, tree) mélèze *(m)*
larder *n* garde-manger *(m)*
large tooth saw *n* scie *(f)* grosse coupe
latch *n* loquet *(m)*
(auto ~) loquet *(m)* automatique
(door ~) loquet *(m)* à poucier;
(gate ~) platine *(f)* pivotante
(stirrup ~) loquet *(m)* étrier
latch (to) *v* fermer au loquet
latching lock *n* serrure *(f)* de sûreté
lath *n* latte *(f)*

Lathe   # Length

lathe *n* **(wood turning ~)** tour *(m)* à bois
(metalwork ~) tour *(m)* à métaux
lattice *n*   treillis *(m)*
lattice girder *n*   poutre *(f)* en treillis
lattice window *n*   fenêtre *(f)* à croisillons de plomb
laundry room *n*   buanderie *(f)*
lavatory *n*   toilettes *(fpl)*
lawn *n* (cut grass) pelouse *(f)*
lawnmower *n*   tondeuse *(f)*
(motor ~) tondeuse *(f)* à moteur
(electric ~)   tondeuse *(f)* électrique
lawyer *n*   avocat / e *(m)/(f)*
lay (to) *v* (carpet etc.) poser
layer *n* (of paint, plaster etc.) couche *(f)*
lead *n* (elec. cable) fil *(m)*
lead *n* (metal) plomb *(m)*
lead *n* (for windows) baguette *(f)* de plomb
lead pencil *n*   crayon *(m)* à papier
leaded lights *npl*   petits carreaux *(mpl)* d'une fenêtre
leaded window *n*   fenêtre *(f)* à petits carreaux
lead free *adj*   sans plomb
leak *n* (in roof; tank; pipe) fuite *(f)*
(gas ~) une fuite *(f)* de gaz
leak (to) *v*   fuir; ('escape' from container, tank) échapper
lean-to *n* (hut, garage, shed) en appentis *(m)*
lease *n*   bail *(m)*
lease holder *n*   locataire *(m)/(f)* à bail
leather *n*   cuir *(m)*; **(wash ~)** *n*   peau *(f)* de chamois
LED (light emitting diode) *n*   DEL (diode *(f)* électroluminescente)
leg *n* (furniture) pied *(m)*
legal *adj*   légal
legal (is it ~ to do?)   est il légal de faire?
legal (to seek ~ advice)   consulter un avocat
length *n*   longueur *(f)*

Length – Conversion table

Imperial Measure (UK) - Metric

1 inch (in.) = 2.54 centimetre (cm.)
1 foot (ft.) = 30.48 cm.
1 yard (yd.) = 91.44 cm.
1 mile (ml.) (1760 yd.) = 1.61 kilometre (km.)
= (1610 metre (m.)

Metric - Imperial Measure (UK)

1 millimetre (mm.) = 0.04 inch (in,)
1 centimetre (cm.) = 0.39 in.
1 metre (m.) = 39.37 in.
= 3.28 foot (ft.)
= 1.09 yard (yd.)
1 kilometre = 0.62 ml. (1094 yd.)

---

lengthen (to) *v* (objects) prolonger
lengthsman (road ~) *n* **cantonnier** *(m)*
lengthways *adj/adv* dans le sens de la longueur
lens *n* (magnifying glass) loupe *(f)*
lessee *n* (holder of lease) preneur (euse) *(m)/(f)*
lessor *n* (person granting lease) bailleur (eresse) *(m)/(f)*
let *n* (contract) bail *(m)*
let (to) *v* (property) louer
let (to ~) *n* (sign) à louer
letter box *n* boîte *(f)* au lettres
letting *n* (property) location *(f)*
level *n* (gen.) niveau *(m);* (tool) niveau *(m);*
(spirit ~) niveau *(m)* à bulle
level *adj* (household fittings e.g. shelf) droit; (horizontal) horizontal; (surface) plan; (garden, ground) plat
level (to) *v* (knock down) raser
level out (to) *v* (land) s'aplanir
lever *n* levier *(m);* (small) manette *(f)*
lift *n* ascenseur *(m)*
lift (to) *v* soulever
light *n* lumière *(f)*

light *adj* (room, colour) clair; (of little weight) léger (ère)
light indicator *n* (on switch, appliance) voyant *(m)*
light (to) *v* (flame, fire) allumer; (illuminate) éclairer

Light bulb

light bulb *n* ampoule *(f)*

bayonet cap ~ : ampoule culot 'B'
Edison screw cap ~ : ampoule culot 'E'
energy saving ~ : ampoule économie d'énergie
fluorescent tube *n* tube *(m)* fluorescente
fluorescent tube holder *n* réglette *(f)* fluorescente
halogen lamp *n* lampe halogène
incandescent ~ : ampoule incandescente
neon *n* (light) **:** néon *(m)*
screw cap ~ : ampoule à vis

---

light emitting diode (LED) *n* diode *(f)* électroluminescente (DEL)
light switch *n* interrupteur *(m)*; (fam.) inter
lighting *n* (gen.) éclairage *(m)*
lightning *n* éclairs *(mpl)*
lightning conductor *n* paratonnerre *(m)*
lightning strike *n* foudre *(f)*
lignum vitae *n* (wood, tree) gaïac *(m)*
lilac *n/adj* (shrub, colour) lilas *(m)*
lime *n* (calcium) chaux *(f)*; (tree) tilleul *(m)*
(slaked ~) chaux *(f)* éteinte
lime (to) *v* (land) chauler
lime green *n/adj* (colour) citron *(m)inv* vert
lime kiln *n* four *(m)* à chaux
lime pit *n* plain *(m)*
lime scale *n* tarter *(m)*
limestone *n* calcaire *(m)*
lime wash *n* badigeon *(m)*

lime wash (to) *v* blanchir à la chaux
line *n* (to define position) ligne *(f);* (row of people,
cars) file *(f);* (rope) corde *(f);* (phone, elec.) ligne
(f)
line up (to) *v* aligner
linen *n* (textile) lin *(m)*
(household ~) linge *(m)*
linen cupboard *n* armoire *(f)* à linge
liner *n* (of chimney) chemise *(f)*
liner *n* (swimming pool) revêtement *(m)* de
piscine; (swimming pool or garden pond) liner *(m)*
lining paper *n* (wallpaper) papier *(m)* d'apprêt
lino *n* lino *(m)*
linoleum *n* linoléum *(m)*
linseed oil *n* huile *(f)* de lin
lintel *n* linteau *(m)*
liquefied petroleum gas (LPG) *n* gaz *(mpl)*
de pétrole liquéfiés (GPL)
liquid *n* liquide *(m)*
L-iron *n* fer *(m)* en équerre
list price *n* prix *(m)* au catalogue
listed building *n* bâtiment *(m)* classé;
monument *(m)* historique
live *adj* (elec. circuit) sous tension;
(elec. wire) **fil** *(m)* sous tension
living room *n* salon *(m)*
load *n* (stuff to be carried) charge *(f);* (contents of
vehicle) chargement *(m)*
load bearing *adj* porteur (euse) *(m)/(f)*
load bearing wall *n* mur *(m)* portant
lobby *n* (of house) entrée *(f)*
locate (to) *v* (find) retrouver
location *n* (place, district) endroit *(m)*

Lock

lock *n* (key operated ~) serrure *(f)*
lock *n* (secured with bolt) verrou *(m)*

cylinder ~ : barillet *(m)*
deadlock : verrou *(m)* haut sécurité;
verrou *(m)* **à clé**
double lock : (high security) verrou *(m)* de
sûreté
mortise ~ : serrure *(f)* encastrée
Yale ® ~ : serrure *(f)* de sûreté

---

lock (to) *v* (with key) fermer à clé ; (bolt)
verrouiller
locksmith *n* serrurier *(m)*
loft *n* (attic) grenier *(m)*
loft conversion *n* (planning / in progress)
aménagement *(m)* de grenier
loft (habitable ~) *n* grenier *(m)* aménagé
loft hatch *n* trappe *(f)* (du grenier)
loft ladder *n* (gen.) échelle *(f)* d'accès;
(collapsible ~) échelle accordéon;
(retractable ~) échelle escamotable
(sliding ~) échelle coulissante
loggia *n* loggia *(f)*
long *adj* (gen.) long (longue) *(m)/(f)*; **(a ~
time)** longtemps
long handled *adj* à manche long
longways *adv* dans le sens de la longueur
look at (to) *v* (gen.) regarder; (carefully)
examiner
look for (to) *v* chercher;
look in (to) *v* (pass by) passer
look over (cast a glance over / at...) jeter un
coup d'œil sur / à .....
look through (to) *v* (instructions, dictionary)
consulter
looking glass *n* miroir *(m)*; glace *(f)*
loose *adj* (items not pre-packed, sand, chippings
etc.) en vrac

loose *adj* (not firmly fixed) mal fixé; (screw) desserré; (nail, peg) branlant; (joint) lâche
loosen (to) *v* (most fixtures) desserrer
lorry *n* camion *(m)*
(heavy ~) poids *(m)* lourd
(artic. / articulated ~) semi. / semi-remorque *(m)*
lorry driver *n* routier *(m)*; chauffeur *(m)* de poids lourd
lose (to) *v* (mislay) perdre
lost *adj* perdu
losthead *n* (floor nail) clou *(m)* à tête perdue; clou *(m)* sans tête
lot *n* (in auction) lot *(m)*
lot (a ~) *pron* (large quantity) beaucoup; (everything) tout
lounge *n* (of house, flat) salon *(m)*
lounge suite *n* (furniture) sièges *(mpl)* de salon
louse *n* (insect) pou *(m)*
louvre *n* (single element) lame *(f)* persienne
louvred door *n* porte *(f)* persiennée
louvres *n* (in window) vasistas *(m)*
low *adj* bas, basse *(m)/(f)*
low budget *adj* à petit budget
lower (to) *v* baisser
low priced *adj* à bas prix
low voltage *n* basse tension *(f)*
low voltage *adj* de basse tension
LPG *n* **(liquefied petroleum gas)** GPL (gaz de pétrole liquefies) *(mpl)*
lubricant *n* (= grease) graisse *(f)*
lubricating oil *n* huile *(f)* de graissage
lubrication *n* (general) lubrification *(f)*; (engines, machines) graissage *(m)*
lukewarm *adj* tiède

Macerator   Mantelpiece

macerator *n* pompe *(f)* de relevage
machete *n* machette *(f)*
machine *n* (gen.) machine *(f)*
machine for doing .... machine à faire .....
magenta *n/adj* (colour) magenta *(m)inv*
magnet *n* aimant *(m)*
magnetic *adj* aimanté
magnetic compass *n* boussole *(f)*
magnetic storm *n* orage *(m)*
magnify (to) *v* grossir
magnifying glass *n* loupe *(f)*
mahogany *n/adj* (wood, tree, colour) acajou *(m)*
main fuse *n* fusible *(m)* principal
main switch *n* interrupteur *(m)* différentiel
main switchboard *n* tableau *(m)* de
commande
mains *npl* **electricity** électricité *(f)* du secteur
mains *npl* **gas** gaz *(m)* de ville
mains *npl* **water** eau *(f)* courant
mains voltage *n* tension *(f)* de secteur
maintenance *n* entretien *(m)*
maintenance contract *n* contrat *(m)*
d'entretien
maintenance fees *npl* frais *(mpl)* d'entretien
maintenance man *n* ouvrier *(m)* chargé de
l'entretien
make *n* (trademark) marque *(f)*
make (to) *v* (construct) faire; (to a pattern /
design) tailler
mallet *n* maillet *(m)*
manager *n* (person in charge) responsable (job
title) directeur (trice) *(m)/(f)*; gérant (e) *(m)/(f)*
manhole *n* regard *(m)*; bouche *(f)* d'égout;
manhole cover *n* plaque *(f)* de regard
manor *n* manoir *(m)*
manor house *n* maison *(f)* de maître
manse *n* presbytère *(m)*
mansion *n* demeure *(f)*; maison *(f)*
bourgeoise;
mantelpiece / mantelshelf *n* manteau *(m)*
de cheminée

manufacture (to) *v* fabriquer
manufacturer *n* fabricant *(m)*
maple *n* (wood, tree) érable *(m)*
marble *n* (stone, objects) marbre *(m)*
marbling *n* marbrure *(f)*
mark *n* (gen, discoloration) tache *(f)*
mark (to) *v* tacher
market *n* marché *(m)*
maroon *n/adj* (colour) bordeaux *(m)inv*
marsh *n* marécage *(m)*
marshland *n* (wide area) **marais** *(m);* (more
precisely defined) terrain *(m)* marécage
marshy *adj* marécageux (euse)
mask (to) *v* masquer
masking tape *n* ruban *(m)* (adhésif) de
masquage
mason *n* maçon *(m)*
mason's pick *n* smille *(f)*
masonry *n* maçonnerie *(f)*
masonry nail *n* clou *(m)* à béton
masonry paint *n* peinture *(f)* façade
master key *n* passe-partout *(m)inv*
mastic *n* mastic *(m)*
mastic adhesive *n* colle *(f)* mastic
match *n* (fire lighting) allumette *(f)*
matchbox *n* boîte *(f)* d'allumettes
matches (a box of...) *n* une boîte
d'allumettes
material (building ~) *n* matériaux *(mpl)* de
construction
matt *adj* (finish) mat
matt paint *n* peinture *(f)* mate
mattock *n* pioche *(f)* de cantonnier
mauve *n/adj* (colour) mauve *(m)inv*
maximum *n* maximum *(m)*
Mayor *n* maire *(m)*
MDF (medium density fibreboard) *n*
lamifié *(m)*
measure (to) *v* mesurer
measurement *n* dimension *(f)*
measuring tape *n* mètre *(m)* ruban

Measure it!

Those of us who still think instinctively in feet, inches, stones and pounds etc. have probably reached a dignified maturity.
For us this volume includes conversion tables under 'Area', 'Length', 'Volume' and 'Weight'. Even so before ordering any product it is as well to measure the required dimensions or properties in metric units. To add a belt to the braces write them down clearly for presentation to the salesperson.

Mechanic   **Mid price**

mechanic *n* mécanicien (ienne) *(m)/(f)*
mechanism *n* mécanisme *(m)*
medium density fibreboard (MDF) *n* lamifié *(m)*
meeting *n* rencontre *(f)*
melamine *n* mélamine *(f)*
melt (to) *v* faire fondre
melting point *n* point *(m)* de fusion
membrane *n* membrane *(f)*
mend (to) *v* réparer
mercury *n* mercure *(m)*
mesh *n* (fabric) filet *(m);* (metal) grillage *(m)*
metal *n* métal *(m)*
metal bar *n* barre *(f)* en métal
metal frame *n* (for partition) ossature *(f)* métallique
metal household fittings *npl* ferrures *(fpl)*
metal rail *n* (for partition) rail *(m)* métallique
metal sheet *n* tôle *(f)*
metalwork *n* ferronnerie *(f)*
meter *n* (gas, elec. etc.) compteur *(m)*
methylated spirit *n* alcool *(m)* à brûler
metre *n* (length) mètre *(m)* (= 39.37in.; = 3ft. 3.37in.; = 1.09yd.)
metric *adj* métrique
mica *n* mica *(m)*
mid price (at a ~) *n* à prix *(m)* modéré

mill *n* moulin *(m)*
(water ~) moulin *(m)* à eau
(wind ~) moulin *(m)* à vent
mine *n* (ore extraction) mine *(f)*
mineral *n* minéral *(m)*
minimum *n* minimum *(m)*
mining area *n* région *(f)* d'exploitation minière
mirror *n* miroir *(m); glace (f)*
mitre (to) *v* tailler d'onglet
mitre box *n* boîte *(f)* à onglets
mitre joint *n* assemblage *(m)* à onglet
mitre saw *n* scie *(f)* à onglet
mix (to) *v* (combine) mélanger; (cement; mortar etc.) malaxer
mixer *n* (cement) bétonnière *(f)*
mixer tap *n* robinet *(m)* mélangeur
mobile home *n* mobile home *(m)*
mobile shop *n* commerce *(m)* ambulant
modern *adj* moderne
modernise (to) *v* moderniser
moisture *n* humidité *(f)*
monkey wrench *n* clé *(f)* à molette
mortar *n* mortier *(m)*
(dry mixed ~) mortier *(m)* prêt à l'emploi
mortise / mortice *n* mortaise *(f)*
mortise and tenon joint *n* assemblage *(m)* à tenon et mortaise
mortise lock *n* serrure *(f)* encastrée
mosaic *n* mosaïque *(f)*
moss *n* mousse *(f)*
moss covered *adj* moussu
moss green *n/adj* (colour) vert *(m)* mousse *inv*
motor *n* (engine) moteur *(m)*
motor mower *n* tondeuse *(f)* à moteur
mould *n* moisissure *(f)*
moulding *n* (decorative feature) moulure *(f)*
mouse *n* souris *(f)*
mouse hole *n* trou *(m)* de souris
mousetrap *n* souricière *(f)*
move house (to) *v* déménager

moving house *n* **déménagement** *(m)*
mower *n* **(lawn ~)**   tondeuse *(f)* *(à gazon)*
mud *n*   boue *(f)*
mullion *n*   meneau *(m)*
multiple socket adapter *n* (elec.) bloc *(m)*
multiprise
multi purpose saw *n*   scie *(f)* égoïne
universelle
muslin *n*   étamine *(f)*

Nail

nail *n* clou *(m); pointe (f)*

annulated / ring shank ~ : clou annelé
brad (floor ~) : clou à tête perdue
clout ~ (galvanised) **:** clou pour toiture
(galvanisé)
galvanised ~ : clou galvanisé
losthead floor ~ : clou à tête perdue;
clou sans tête
masonry ~ : clou béton
oval wire ~ : clou tête d'homme
panel pin *n* **(fine ~) :** goujon *(m)*
roofing ~ (galvanised) **:** clou pour toiture
(galvanisé)
round wire ~ : clou à tête plat
striated (masonary) **:** clou striés
tack *n* (tin-tack) : clou
tack *n* **(upholstery ~) :** semence *(f)*
threaded (wire) **~ :** clou torsadé

---

nail (to) *v* clouer
nail punch *n* chasse clou *(m)*
nailless / screwless adhesive *n* colle *(f)*
ni-clou ni-vis
name plate *n* (of house) plaque *(f)*
negative *n* (elec. polarity) négatif *(m)*

neon *n* (light) néon *(m)*
neoprene adhesive *n* colle *(f)* néoprène
net *n* (general) filet *(m)*
network *n* (utilities, transport) réseau *(m)*
neutral *adj* (elec. polarity) neutre
new *adj* (experience) nouveau (elle) *(m)/(f);*
(brand ~) neuf / neuve *(m)/(f)*
no sale *n* non-vente *(f)*
noise *n* bruit *(m)*
noiseless *adj* silencieux (ieuse) *(m)/(f)*
noisy *adj* (place, machine) bruyant
nook *n* (cosy corner) coin *(m);* (for ornaments
etc.) niche *(f)*
norm *n* norme *(f)*
normal *n* normale *(f)*
north *n* nord *(m)*
north facing *adj* exposé au nord
north side *n* (land; wall) du côté *(m)* nord
nosing *n* (stair-tread edge) bord arrondi *(m)*
notary *n* (≈ solicitor) notaire *(m)* (term of address
for Notaire) Maître *n(m)* ≈ Sir / Master
notch *n* (cut in wood etc.) entaille *(f)*
notch (to) *v* (to mark) encocher
note *n* (written record) note *(f)*
note (to) *v* noter
notebook *n* (gen.) carnet *(m)*
noted *pp/adj* (s'thing registered / recorded - an
appointment, order for goods etc.) noté
notice *n* (sign) pancarte *(f)*
notice *n* (warning; instruction) préavis *(m)*
nozzle *n* (pipe; tool) jet *(m);* ajutage *(m)*
number *n* (figure) nombre *(m);* (house; tel; credit
card) numéro *(m)*
nut *n* (and bolt) écrou *(m);*
(wing ~) écrou *(m)* à oreilles

oak *n* (wood, tree) chêne *(m)*
(dark ~) (wood, colour) chêne *(m)* foncé
(light ~) (wood, colour) chêne *(m)* clair
oakum *n* étoupe *(f)*
oblong *n* rectangle *(m)*
oblong *adj* oblong (ongue) (m)/(f);
rectangulaire
occupation *n* métier *(m)*
ochre *n/adj* (colour) ocre *(m)*
odd job *n* (for cash) petit bulot *(m);*
(household) bricoler dans la maison
odds and ends *npl* bricoles *(fpl)*
odour *n* odeur *(f)*
odourless *adj* inodore
off = not functioning (water, gas) coupé;
(tap) fermé; (elec. appliances) éteint
off-centre *adj* décentré
office *n* (room) bureau *(m);* cabinet *(m)* (gen.;
small; an agency including Estate Agency e.g.
Cabinet Véronique, Agent immobilier)
oil *n* (lubricating) huile *(f);* (heating) fioul *(m);*
mazout *(m)*
oil drum *n* citerne *(f)* à pétrole
oil gauge *n* jauge *(f)* de niveau d'huile
oil lamp *n* lampe *(f)* à pétrole
oil tank *n* (domestic) cuve *(f)*
oil based *adj* (paint) à base d'huile
oilcan *n* burette *(f)* d'huile
oilcloth *n* toile (f) cirée
oil fired *adj* (heating etc.) au fioul
oilstone *n* pierre *(f)* à aiguiser
open *adj* (opp. to 'closed') ouvert
open (to) *v* ouvrir
open air *adj* en plein air
opening *n* ouverture *(f)*
opening hours *n* (of shops etc.) heures
(fpl) d'ouverture
open plan *adj* (office) paysager (ère)
operating instructions *npl* mode *(m)*
d'emploi
opposite *n* contraire *(m)*

Opposite   Owner

opposite *n* (the exact ~) tout le contraire
orange *n/adj* (colour) orange *(m)inv*
orchard *n* verger *(m)*
order *n* (commission) commande *(f)*
order (to) *v* commander
order book *n* carnet *(m)* de commandes
order form *n* bon *(m)* de commande
order number *n* numéro *(m)* de commande
order to view *n* permis *(m)* de visiter
ornament (to) *v* (building, structure) orner
outbuilding *n* dépendance *(f)*
outdoor *adj* de plein air
outdoor *adv* dehors; à l'extérieur; (on patio or formal area) à la terrasse
outlet connector *n* (wash basin) raccord *(m)* sortie lavabo
outlet valve *n* soupape *(f)* d'échappement
outline *n* (gen, idea) idée *(f); bref exposé *(m)*
outline (to) *v* (give the gen. idea) exposer brièvement
outside *n* (of property) extérieur *(m); (patio or formal area) terrasse *(f)*
outside *adv* dehors; à l'extérieur
oval *adj* (shape) ovale
oven *n* four *(m)*
overalls *npl* (boilersuit) bleu *(m)* de travail; (dungarees) salopette *(f)*
overestimate *n* surestimation *(f)*
overflow pipe *n* tuyau *(m)* de trop-plein
overflowing *adj* (bath; sink; d'bin) débordant
overfull *n* (sink, bath etc.) trop-plein *(m)*
overhang *n* (of eaves) avancée *(f)*
overhanging *adj* surplomb
overhead *adv* (above head level) au dessus
overhead light *n* plafonnier *(m)*
overlap (to) *v* recouvrir partiellement
overload *n* (elec., gen.) surcharge *(f)*
overload (to) *v* surcharger
overmantel *n* trumeau *(m)*
owner *n* propriétaire *(m)/(f)*

pack (to) *v* (place in carton etc) emballer
package *n*   colis *(m);* paquet *(m)*
packaging *n*   emballage *(m)*
packet *n*   paquet *(m)*
packing *n*   emballage *(m)*
pad *n* (support, protect) protection *(f)*
pad saw *n*   scie *(f)* à guichet
padded *adj* (material) rembourré
padding *n*   rembourrage *(m)*
paddock *n*   paddock *(m);* enclos *(m);*
padlock *n*   cadenas *(m);* (long shackle)
cadenas *(m)* anse haute
padlock (to) *v*   cadenasser
pail *n*   seau *(m)*

Paint - and paintwork

paint *n*   peinture *(f)*

coat *n* (of paint) couche *(f)* (de peinture)
eggshell finish ~ : peinture coquille d'œuf
emulsion ~ : peinture émulsion
enamel ~ : peinture laquée
gloss ~ : peinture brillante
masonry ~ : peinture façade
matt ~ : peinture mate
oil based ~ : peinture à base d'huile
primer *n*   apprêt *(m)*
primer (stabilising ~) *n* durcisseur *(m)* pour plâtre
satin ~ : peinture satinée
shellac varnish *n* gomme-laque *(f)*
silk finish ~ : peinture satinée
undercoat *n* (paint) couche *(f)* de fond
varnish *n*   vernis *(m)*

Paint colours

azure azur *(m)*
beige beige *(m)*
black noir *(m); *(jet ~)* n* noir *(m)* d'ébène
bronze couleur *(f)* de bronze *(m)*
brown marron *(m)*
burnt sienna terre *(f)* de Sienne brûlée
burnt umber terre *(f)* d'ombre brûlée
cherry rouge cerise *inv*
copper cuivre *(m)*
crimson cramoisi *(m)*
ebony noir *(m)* d'ébène
eggshell blue bleu *(m)* pâle
emerald green vert *(m)* émeraude
flame-coloured rouge feu *inv*
grey gris *(m)*
ivory ivoire *(m)*
jade vert *(m)* jade
lilac lilas *(m)*
lime green citron (m) vert *inv*
magenta magenta
mahogany acajou *(m)*
maroon bordeaux *(m)*
mauve mauve *(m)inv*
moss green vert *(m)inv* mousse
oak chêne *(m)*
oak (dark) chêne *(m)* foncé
oak (light) chêne *(m)* clair
ochre ocre
orange orange *inv*
powder blue bleu *(m)* pastel
puce rouge-brun *inv*
purple (reddish) pourpre
purple (bluish) violet
red rouge
rose-red vermeil (eille) *(m)/(f)*
ruby rouge *(m)* rubis
rust-coloured couleur rouille *inv*
scarlet écarlate *(f)*
shocking pink rose *(m)* vif
silver argent *(m)*

Paint Colours (continued).

slate blue bleu *(m)* ardoise
slate grey gris *(m)* ardoise
steel blue bleu *(m)/inv* acier
terracotta ocre brun *(m)*
turquoise turquoise *(f)*
violet violet (ette) *(m)/(f)*
white blanc *(m)*
yellow jaune *(m)*
yellow ochre jaune d'ocre *(m)*

Useful terms:

dark foncé
darker plus foncé
light clair
lighter plus clair
pale pâle
shade ton *(m)*

Paint   Pane

paint (to) *v* peindre
paint pot *n* pot *(m)* de peinture
paint remover *n* (chemical) décapant *(m);*
(tool) racloir *(m)*
paint roller *n* rouleau *(m)* à peinture
paint spray *n* peinture *(f)* en aérosol; bombe
(f) de peinture
paint spraygun *n* pistolet *(m)* à peinture
paint stripper *n* (chemical) décolleuse *(f)* de
peint; (tool) racloir *(m)*
paint tray *n* bac *(m)* à peinture
paintbrush *n* brosse *(f);* pinceau *(m)*
painter *n* peintre *(m)*
painter decorator *n* peintre décorateur *(m)*
paintwork *n* peintures *(fpl)*
pale *(adj)* (colour) pâle
pan / plate of scales *n* plateau *(m)* de
balance
pane *n* carreau *(m):* vitre *(f)*

panel *n* panneau *(m)*
panel pin *n* (fine nail) goujon *(m)*
panel saw *n* scie *(f)* à panneaux
panelled *adj* (room, fencing etc.) en panneaux;
(door, ceiling) lambrissé; cloisonné
pantry *n* garde manger *(m)*
paperhanging brush *n* brosse *(f)* de
tapissier
paraffin *n* pétrole *(m)*
paraffin wax *n* paraffine *(f)*
parapet *n* parapet *(m)*
parasite *n* parasite *(m)*
parcel *n* colis *(m)*; paquet *(m)*
parlour *n* petit salon *(m)*
parquet *n* parquet *(m)*
partition *n* cloison *(f)*
partition wall *n* cloison *(f)*
party wall *n* mur *(m)* mitoyen
passage *n* (interior) corridor *(m)*; (exterior)
passage *(m)*
passkey *n* passe *(m)*
paste *n* (mixture) pâte *(f)*; (glue) colle *(f)*; (for
wallpaper) colle *(f)* à papier peint
paste (to) *v* (wallpaper etc.) encoller;
pasting table *n* table *(f)* à tapissier
pasture *n* (grassland) pré *(m)*; pâturage *(m)*
path / pathway *n* chemin *(m)*; (narrow)
sentier *(m)*
patio *n* terrasse *(f)*; patio *(m)*
patio doors *npl* porte fenêtre *(f)*
pattern *n* (template) modèle *(m)*
pave (to) *v* paver
paved *adj* pavé
paving *n* dalles *(fpl)*
paving stone *n* dalle *(f)*
pay *n* (to general worker) paie *(f)*; (professional)
salaire *(m)*
pay (to) *v* payer
payment *n* paiement *(m)*; (to settle account)
règlement *(m)*

pebbledash *n* crépi *(m)* gravillonné;
mouchetis *(m)*
pebbledash (to) *v* crépir
pedestal *n* (statue) piédestal *(m)*; socle *(m)*;
(wash basin) colonne *(f)*
pedestal washbasin *n* lavabo colonne *(f)*
peg *n* (for awning, tent) piquet *(m)*
pelmet *n* cantonnière *(f)*
permission *n* **(planning ~)** permis *(m)* de
construire
Perspex ® *n* plexiglas ® *(m)*
Phillips ® **screwdriver** *n* tournevis *(m)* pour
vis Philips ®
photo electric cell *n* cellule *(f)*
photoélectrique
pick *n* (tool) pioche *(f)*; pic *(m)*
(mason's ~) smille *(f)*
pickaxe *n* pioche *(f)* hache
pigsty *n* porcherie *(f)*
pillar *n* pilier *(m)*
pilot light *n* lampe *(f)* témoin
pin *n* (to attach paper, textiles) épingle *(f)*; (of
elec. plug) fiche *(f)*
(safety ~) épingle *(f)* de sûreté
(upholstery ~) clou *(m)* tapissier
(panel ~) (fine nail) goujon *(m)*
pincers *n* pince *(f)*
pine *n* (wood, tree) pin *(m)*
(stripped ~) (timber) pin *(m)* décapé
pipe *n* tuyau *(m)*; tube *(m)*
(copper ~) tuyau / tube *(m)* cuivre
(plastic ~) tuyau / tube *(m)* plastique
pipe bend *n* coude *(m)* de tube
pipe bending spring *n* ressort *(m)* à cintrer
pipe clip *n* collier *(m)* simple
pipe cutter *n* (tool) coupe-tube *(m)*;
molette *(f)* coupante

Pipe fittings

collar *n* (on pipework) bague *(f)*
compression joint / connector *n* raccord *(m)* instantané
compression joint / connector *n* (for metal pipes with 'olive' seals) raccord *(m)* à olive
connector *n* raccord *(m)*
(angle ~) raccord courbe
(elbow ~) raccord coude
(lengthy flexible ~) flexible *(m)* d'alimentatuin
(straight ~) raccord droit
connector (straight reducing ~) raccord droit (réduction)
drain tap *n* robinet *(m)* de vidange
plug *n* (pipe end closure) bouchon *(m)*
soldered joint / connector *n* raccord *(m)* à souder
straight connector *n* manchon *(m)*
'T' joint *n* (all equal diam.) raccord *(m)* té égal
'T' joint *n* (various diam.) raccord *(m)* té inégal
union *n* (threaded connector) union *(f)*

pipe wrench *n* serre tubes *(m)*
pipework *n* canalisation *(f)*
pipework (waste ~) *n* canalisations *(fpl)* d'évacuation
pitch *n* (tar) brai *(m)*
pitchfork *n* fourche *(f)*
pitch pine *n* (wood, tree) pichpin *(m)*
plan *n* plan *(m)*
plane *n* (wood ~) (tool) rabot *(m)*
planed wood *n* bois *(m)* raboté
plank *n* planche *(f)*
planking *n* planches *(fpl)*
planning permission *n* permis *(m)* de construire
planning regulations *npl* règlements *(mpl)* d'urbanisme
plaster *n* plâtre *(m)*

Plaster   **Pointing trowel**

plaster (to) *v* faire les plâtres
plaster of Paris *n* plâtre *(m)* de Paris
plasterboard *n* plaque *(f)* de plâtre;
placoplâtre ® *(m)*
(fireproofed ~) plaque *(f)* de plâtre ignifugée
plasterer *n* plâtrier *(m)*
plasterwork *n* plâtres *(mpl)*
plastic *n* plastique *(m)*
plastic pipe *n* tuyau / tube *(m)* plastique
plate *n* (metal sheet) plaque *(f)*; tôle *(f)*
plate (to) *v* (metal coating) plaquer
plate glass *n* verre *(m)* à vitre
plated *adj* (with precious metal) plaqué
plating *n* (metal coating) placage *(m)*;
(metal ~) protection on doors etc.) tôle *(f)*
pliers *npl* pinces *(fpl)*
(long nose ~) pinces *(f)* à becs de longueur
plinth *n* plinthe *(f)*
plot *n* **(building ~)** terrain *(m)* à bâtir
plug *n* (elec.) fiche *(f)*; (basin, bath etc.) bonde
(f); (Rawlplug ®) cheville *(f)*; (pipe end closure)
bouchon *(m)*
plug (to) *v* (hole etc) boucher
plughole *n* bonde *(f)*
plug in (to) *v* (elec. circuit) brancher
plumb *n* (vertical) à plomb *(m)*
plumb line *n* fil *(m)* à plomb
plumber *n* plombier *(m)*
plumber's merchant *n* grossiste *(m)* en
plomberie
plumbing *n* plomberie *(f)*
plunger *n* (unblocking drains) ventouse *(f)*
plunger pump *n* (hand pump to unblock drains)
pompe *(f)* hydraulique à main pour déboucher
plywood *n* contreplaqué *(m)*; (three / five ply
etc.) trios / cinq plis etc.
point (to) *v* (brickwork etc.) jointoyer
pointing *n* (brickwork etc.) jointoyer *(m)*; (more
fam.) joints *(mpl)*
pointing iron *n* fer *(m)* à jointoyer
pointing trowel *n* truelle *(f)* à joints

pole *n* perche *(f)*
(flag ~) mât *(m)*
polish *n* (for wood) cire *(f);* (metal) pâte *(f)* à polir
polish (to) *v* (furniture etc) cirer; (metal, glass) astiquer; (marble; stone) polir
polystyrene *n* polystyrène *(m)*
(expanded ~) polystyrène *(m)* expansé
polystyrene cement *n* colle *(f)* polystyrène
polystyrene chips *npl* billes *(fpl)* de polystyrène
polythene *n* polyéthylène *(m)*
polyurethane *n* polyuréthane *(m)*
pond *n* (garden) basin; (larger) étang *(m)*
pool *n* **(swimming ~)** piscine *(f)*
pool liner *n* revêtement *(m)* de piscine; liner *(m)*
poplar *n* (wood, tree) peuplier *(m)*
porch *n* porche *(m)*
portico *n* portique *(m)*
positive *n* (elec. polarity) positif *(m)*
post *n* (pole) poteau *(m)*
(fence ~) piquet *(f)* de clôture
post (to) *v* (send by ~) poster; expédier; (place in post box) mettre à la poste; (display notice etc.) afficher
post box *n* boîte *(f)* aux lettres
post holder / sole plate *n* (metal) semelle *(f)*
(metal, bolt fixed ~) semelle *(f)* boulonnée
(with metal stake ~) semelle *(f)* sur piquet métallique
pot *n* (paint etc.) pot *(m)*
pots and pans *n* casseroles *(fpl)*
powder blue *n/adj* (colour) bleu *(m)* pastel
power *n* (elec.) énergie *(f)* électrique
power cut *n* coupure *(f)* de courant
power line *n* ligne *(f)* à haute tension
power point *n* prise *(f)* (de courant)
power saw *n* scie *(f)* électrique
power supply *n* alimentation *(f)* de secteur
power tool *n* outil *(m)* électrique

powered screwdriver *n* visseuse *(f)*
preservation order *n* **(the house has a ~)**
la maison est classé
preservation order *v* **(to apply a ~)** classer
preservative *n* (for timber) revêtement *(m)*
protecteur
preserve (to) *v* préserver
pressure *n* pression *(f)*
pressure gauge *n* manomètre *(m);* indicateur
(m) de pression
price *n* prix *(m)*
price list *n* liste *(f)* des prix
primer *n* apprêt *(m)*
primer *n* **(stabilising ~)** durcisseur *(m)* pour
plâtre
propane *n* propane *(m)*
property *n* (buildings; land etc.) biens *(mpl);*
(buildings) immobiliers *(mpl)*
PTFE tape *n* ruban *(m)* Téflon ® d'étanchéité
puce *adj* (colour) rouge brun *inv*
pull down *v* (building, property) abattre
pump *n* pompe *(f)*
(circulating ~) pompe *(f)* de circulation
(heat ~) pompe *(f)* à chaleur
pump (to) *v* pomper
punch *n* (timber, metal) perçoir *(m);* (for
leather) alène *(f)*
punch (to) *v* (make a hole with hand tool)
poinçonner
purchase *n* (buy) achat *(m)*
purchase (to) *v* acheter
purchaser *n* acheteur (euse) *(m)/(f)*
purlin *n* panne *(f)*
purple *adj* (colour) (reddish) pourpre; (bluish)
violet
push button *n* bouton *(m)* poussoir
put (to) *v* mettre
put in place (to) *v* poser
putty *n* mastic *(m)*
putty (to) *v* mastiquer

quarry *n* (stone extraction) carrière *(f)*
quarry (to) *v* (extract stone etc.) extraire
quarry tile *n* carreau *(m)* de terre
quarter *n* (1/4) quart *(m)*
quartz *n* (mineral) quartz *(m)*
quote *n* (estimate) devis *(m)*

Rabbet   **Real estate**

rabbet *n* rainure *(f)*
rabbet plane *n* guillaume *(m)*
rack *n* (storage) étagère *(f)*
radiator *n* (heating) radiateur *(m)*
radius *n* rayon *(m)*
rafter *n* chevron *(m)*
rag *n* (cloth) chiffon *(m)*
rail *n* **(curtain ~)** tringle *(f)*
(balcony ~) balustrade *(f)*
(fencing ~) barreau *(m)*
(hand ~) rampe *(f)*
(metal ~) (for partition) rail *(m)* métallique
ramin *n* (timber) ramin *(m)*
ramp *n* (in gen., access) rampe *(f)*
rasp *n* (tool) râpe *(f)*
rasp (to) *v* grincer
rat *n* rat *(m)*
ratchet *n* (rack) crémaillère *(f)*
ratchet wheel *n* roue *(f)* à rochet
Rawlplug ®; Rawlbolt ® *n* cheville *(f)*
razor *n* rasoir *(m)*
razor blade *n* lame *(f)* de rasoir
razor wire *n* feuillard *(m)*
RCD (residual current device) *n* disjoncteur
(m) différentiel
ready mix concrete *n* béton *(m)* pré mélangé
ready-to-mix *adj* (dry mix) prêt à gâcher
real estate *n* biens *(mpl);* immobiliers *(mpl)*
real estate agent *n* agent *(m)* immobilier
rebuild (to) *v* reconstruire

rebuilding *n* reconstruction *(f)*
reconstruct (to) *v* reconstruire
reconstruction *n* reconstruction *(f)*
red *n/adj* (colour) rouge *(m)*
redecorate (to) *v* réaménager; (paintwork & wallpaper) repeindre et retapisser
redecoration *n* travaux *(mpl)* de peinture
refurbish (to) *v* rénover
refuse *n* (rubbish) (domestic) ordures *(fpl);* **(garden ~)** déchets *(mpl)* de jardinage
refuse bin *n* poubelle *(f)*
refuse chute *n* vide ordures *(fpl)*
refuse disposal unit *n* broyeur *(m)* d'ordures
refuse dump *n* déchetterie *(f)*
regulations (planning ~) *npl* règlement *(mpl)* d'urbanisme
reinforced concrete *n* béton *(m)* armé
reinforcement *n* (in buildings, concrete) armature *(f)*
reinforcing plate *n* plaque *(f)* renfort
remote control *n* (unit) télécommande *(f)*
remote gate control *n* motorisation *(f)* de porte / portail
removal *n* (moving home) déménagement *(m)*
removal van *n* camion *(m)* de déménagement
remover *n* (occupation) déménageur *(m)*
render (to) *v* (wall etc.) enduire; crépir
rendered *adj* crépi
rendering *n* (mortar / cement / plaster mix) enduit *(m)*
rendering *n* (surface layer on building) crépi *(m);* **(pebble dash ~)** crépi *(m)* gravillonné **(rough ~)** mouchetis *(m)*
renovate (to) *v* rénover
renovation *n* rénovation *(f)*
rent *n* (for property) loyer *(m)*
rent (to) *v* louer
rental *n* (of property, vehicles) (also fee - for ~) location *(f)*
repaint (to) *v* repeindre

Repair   **Right angle**

repair *n* réparation *(f)*
repair (to) *v* réparer
repair man / woman *n* réparateur (trice) *(m)/(f)*
repairable *adj* réparable
repaper (to) *v* retapisser

Residence

residence *n* (house, home) maison *(f)*

(dwelling, home) demeure *(f)*
(luxury home) maison *(f)* de standing
(family home) maison *(f)* familiale
(family dwelling) demeure *(f)* familiale
(See also: "House and housing p. "

---

restoration *n* (of building) restitution *(f)*

The gastronomy of buildings.

Many language tutors will tell one that words
finishing in '*–ation*' are the same in English
and French. 'Restoration' is (as they say) an
exception that proves the rule. The spoken
word 'restoration' is considered (in French) to
be '*restauration*' meaning the provision of
meals or food. This explains the blank looks
one gets if one talks enthusiastically about the
'restoration' of one's property!

For **'restoration'** use **'restitution'** or play
safe and use **'renovation'** **('rénovation')**.

---

retail centre / park *n* centre *(m)* commercial
revaluation *n* réévaluation *(f)*
revalue (to) *v* réévaluer
rewire (to) *v* refaire l'installation électrique
ridge material *n* faîtage *(m)*
ridge tile *n* tuile *(f)* faîtière; enfaîteau *(m)*
right angle *n* angle *(m)* droit

ridge *n* (roof) faîte *(m);*
right angled *adj* à angle droit
right of way *n* (on a lane, property) droit *(m)* de passage
rimlock *n* (with key and button) verrou *(m)* clé et bouton
ring *n* (circular object) anneau *(m)*
(split ~) anneau *(m)* brise
ring main *n* (elec.) circuit *(m)* principal

Ring main.

The ring main – the standard electrical domestic installation in the UK – is not accepted practice in France. Their regulations require spur lighting and power circuits from the circuit breakers each with no more than five outlets. Somewhat strangely double or even multiple power sockets count as one outlet as does a chandelier at a lighting point.

Competent electricians are known to have re-wired renovated homes to British standards – including square-pinned sockets. It's not as well known what happens when they try to sell the properties to the French or even when the man from EDF comes round!

---

ring spanner *n* clé *(f)* polygonale
rip saw *n* scie *(f)* à refendre
riser *n* (staircase) contremarche *(f)*
rising damp *n* humidité *(f)* s'élevant du sol
rivet *n* (metal fixing) rivet *(m)*
(round head ~) rivet *(m)* à tête ronde
rivet (to) *v* riveter
rock wool *n* laine *(f)* minérale
rod *n* (of wood) tige *(f);* (of metal) tringle *(f);*
(drain ~s) *npl* tiges déboucher *(m)*
roller *n* **(paint ~)** rouleau *(m)* de peintre
roof *n* toit *(m)*
(flat ~) toit terrasse *(m)*

roof (glass ~) verrière *(f)*
roof (to) *v* faire la couverture
roof light *n* fenêtre *(f)* de toit
roof tile *n* tuile *(f)*
roof window *n* fenêtre *(f)* de toit
(dormer ~) lucarne *(f)*
roofer *n* couvreur
roofing *n* (material) toiture *(f);* couverture *(f)*
roofing *n* (putting in place) pose *(f)* de la toiture
roofing felt *n* carton *(m)* bitumé
room *n* (gen.) pièce *(f)*
room divider *n* étagère *(f)* de séparation
rope *n* corde *(f)*
rose *n* (ceiling plaster) rosace *(f);* (shower head)
pomme *(f)* de douche
rose *n/adj* (colour) rose *(m)*
rose window *n* rosace *(f)*
rose red *n/adj* (colour) vermeil (eille) *(m)/(f)*
rosewood *n* (timber) bois *(m)* de rose
rot *n* (decay) pourriture *(f)*
rot (to) *v* (decay) pourrir
rotary clothes line *n* séchoir *(m)* parapluie
rotproof *adj* imputrescible
rotten *adj* (decay) pourri
rotting *adj* (decay) pourrissant
rough *adj* (surface) rêche; (worse) rugueux
(euse) *(m)/(f)*
roughcast *n* mouchetis *(m)*
roughcast *adj* crépi
roughcast (to) *v* crépir
rough hewn *adj* (stone, timber) équarri
roughness *n* rugosité *(f)*
RSJ (rolled steel joist) *n* poutre *(f)* en fer
rubber *n* (substance) caoutchouc *(m);* (eraser)
gomme *(f)*
rubber glove *n* gant *(m)* en caoutchouc
rubber stamp *n* tampon *(m)*
rubbish *n* (waste) ordures *(fpl);* (junk) saletés
(fpl)
rubbish bin *n* poubelle *(f)*
rubbish chute *n* vide ordures *(m)inv*

rubbish collection n ramassage (m) des ordures
rubbish dump / tip n décharge (f) publique
rubble n **(building ~)** gravats (mpl)
ruby n/adj (colour) rouge (m) rubis
ruin n (building) ruine (f)
ruined adj en ruines
rule n (measure) règle (f); **(coiled spring ~)** réglet (f) inox flexible; **(folding ~)** n mesure (f) pliante
rung n (ladder) barreau (m)
rust n rouille (f)
rust coloured adj (colour) couleur rouille inv
rusted adj rouillé
rustic n campagnard (e) (m)/(f)
rustic adj (timber products) rustique; (quaint) champêtre
rust-proof adj (metal) inoxydable; (fam.) inox
rust-proof (to) v traiter contre la rouille
rustproofing n traitement (m) anti-rouille
rusty adj rouillé

sack n (large bag) sac (m)
safe n (secure box) coffre-fort (m)
safety glass n verre (m) de sécurité
safety helmet n casque (m) de protection
safety valve n soupape (f) de sécurité
saleroom n hôtel (m) des ventes
sales rep. / representative n représentant (e) (m)/(f)
salesperson n vendeur (euse) (m)/(f)
sample n échantillon (m)

Sand

sand *n* sable *(m)*

coarse ~ : sable *(m)* grossier
fine ~ : sable *(m)* fin
river ~ : sable *(m)* de rivière
sand (loose, in bulk) : sable *(m)* en vrac
sharp ~ : sable *(m)* liant
silver ~ : sable *(m)* argenté
soft ~ : sable *(m)* doux

---

sand (to) *v* (make smooth) poncer
sandalwood *n* (wood, tree) santal *(m)*
sandbag *n* sac *(m)* de sable
sandblaster *n* (machine) sableuse *(f)*
sandblasting *n* sablage *(m);* décapage *(m)* **au jet de sable**
sanding *n* ponçage *(m)*
sanding block *n* cale *(f)* à poncer
sanding disc *n* disque *(m)* abrasif
sanding machine *n* ponceuse *(f)*
(belt ~) ponceuse à bande
(orbital ~) ponceuse vibrantes
(random orbit ~) ponceuse excentrique
sandpaper *n* papier *(m)* de verre
sandpit *n* (garden) bac *(m)* à sable; (quarry) sablière *(f)*
sandstone *n* grès *(m)*
sanitary *adj* (fittings) sanitaire
sanitation *n* (waste water) assainissement *(m)*
sash lock *n* serrure *(f)* demi-tour
sash window *n* fenêtre *(f)* à guillotine
satellite aerial / dish *n* antenne *(f)* parabolique
satin paint *n* peinture *(f)* satinée
satinwood *n* (wood, tree) bois *(m)* satiné de l'Inde
saw (to) *v* scier
saw blade *n* lame *(f)* de scie

Saw

saw *n* scie *(f)*

band ~ : scie à ruban
carpenters ~ : scie de charpentier
chain ~ : tronçonneuse *(f)*
circular ~ : scie circulaire
coping / fret ~ : scie à chantourner
crosscut ~ : scie de travers
fine tooth ~ : scie à denture américaine
frame ~ : scie à monture de menuisier
hack ~ : scie à métaux
hand ~ : scie égoïne; scie *(f)* manuelle
jig ~ : scie sauteuse
keyhole ~ : scie à guichet
large tooth ~ : scie grosse coupe
mitre ~ : scie à onglet
multi purpose ~ : scie égoïne universelle
pad ~ : scie à guichet
panel ~ : scie à panneaux
power ~ : scie électrique
rip ~ : scie à refendre
scroll ~ : scie à ruban de précision
tenon ~ : scie à dos; scie *(f)* à onglets
trepan *n* **(cylindrical ~)** : trépan *(m)*
veneer ~ : scie à placage

Saw to Size

One of the most useful services commonly available in out-of-town DIY stores in France is that of the 'Saw to Size' centre. They are generally to be found in a corner or at the rear of the building behind an unassuming counter. They use a powerful circular saw on a vertical jig to make short work of cutting wood and timber substitute panels to size. The product is then charged according to its area. Generally operators are reluctant to cut out numerous small components but familiarity and a pleasant manner can work wonders!

sawdust *n* sciure *(f)*
saw edged *adj* à lame dentée
S-bend *n* (plumbing) coud *(m)* en 'S'
scaffold *n* (building) échafaudage *(m)*
scaffold board *n* planche *(f)* d'échafaudage
scaffold tower *n* échafaudage *(m)* tour
scaffolder *n* monteur *(m)* d'échafaudages
scaffolding *n* échafaudage *(m)*
scale *n* (gradations) échelle *(f)*
scale *n* (lime deposit) calcaire *(m)*
scale drawing *n* dessin *(m)* à l'échelle;
scale model *n* maquette *(f)* à l'échelle
scales *npl* (weighing) balance *(f)*
scarlet *n/adj* (colour) écarlate *(f)*
scent *n* (flowers, perfume) parfum *(m)*
scent (to) *n* (flowers, perfume) parfumer
scheme *n* plan *(m)*; projet *(m)*
scissors *npl* ciseaux *(mpl)*
(decorating ~) ciseaux *(mpl)* de décoration
(heavy duty ~) ciseaux *(mpl)* gros travaux
scoop *n* (tool) pelle *(f)*
scrap iron / metal *n* ferraille *(f)*
scrap merchant *n* marchand *(m)* de ferraille
scrap yard *n* chantier *(m)* de ferraille
scrape (to) *v* (clean) gratter; (scratch paintwork etc.) érafler
scraper *n* (decorating etc.) racloir *(m)*
scratch *n* (mark on paintwork etc.) éraflure *(f)*
scratch (to) *v* (make a mark on) érafler
screed *n* (levelling) chape *(f)* de nivellement
screen *n* (to prohibit vision, wind etc.) écran *(m)*:
(folding partition) cloison *(f)* mobile;
screen (to) *v* (hide) cacher; (mask) masquer
screen door *n* porte *(f)* munie d'une moustiquaire

Screw

screw *n* (means of fixing) vis *(f)*;
Allen (hexagonal) socket head ~ : vis à tête six pans
coach ~ : vis tire-fond tête hexagonale
countersunk ~ : vis à tête fraisée
cross head ~ : vis cruciforme
drywall ~ (for plasterboard) : vis trompette
easydrive ~ : vis à tête etoile
grub ~ : vis sans tête
Philips ® ~ : vis Phillips ®
Pozidrive ® ~ : vis Pozidrive ® / Pozi
round head countersunk screw (decorative, used with cup washer) vis à tête fraisée bombée
self tapping ~ : vis auto-perceuse ;
round head ~ : vis à tête ronde
slotted ~ : vis à tête fendue
wood ~ : vis à bois

screw (to) *v* (fix) viser
screw bolt *n* boulon *(m)*

Screwdriver

screwdriver *n* tournevis *(m)*

cross head ~ : tournevis cruciforme
electrician's ~ : tournevis d'électricien
Phillips ® ~ : tournevis pour vis Philips ®
Pozidrive ® ~ : tournevis pour vis Posidrive ®
power ~ : visseuse *(f)*

screwdriver-tester *n* (elec.) tournevis *(m)* testeur
screw eye *n* piton *(m)*
screw hook *n* crochet *(m)* à visser
scroll saw *n* scie *(f)* à ruban de précision
scullery *n* arrière cuisine *(f)*
seal *n* (tight closure) scellé *(m)*

seal (to) *v* sceller
sealant / sealer *n* (coating) enduit *(m)* d'étanchéité
seat *n* (furniture) siège *(m)*
secateurs *npl* sécateur *(m)*
security light *n* **(infrared ~)** lampe *(f)* détecteur infrarouge
security lighting *n* éclairage *(m)* de sécurité
seep (to) *v* (small flow) suinter
seepage *n* (small flow) suintement *(m);* (from fuel tank etc.) fuite *(f);* (drainage to land / water) infiltration *(f)*
self-adhesive *adj* auto-collant
self-tapping screw *n* vis *(m)* auto-perceuse
sell (to) *v* vendre
sell up (to) *v* vendre tout
seller *n* vendeur (euse) *(m)/(f)*
selling *n* vente *(f)*
selling price *n* prix *(m)* de vente
Sellotape ® *n* scotch ® *(m)*
semi-detached *n* (house) maison *(f)* jumelée
sensor *n* détecteur *(m)*
septic tank *n* fosse *(f)* septique
service *n* (maintenance) révision *(f)*
service centre *n* centre *(m)* de service
service charge *n* (maintenance) charges *(fpl)* locatives
service contract *n* contrat *(m)* d'entretien
service engineer *n* technicien *(m)* de maintenance
service hatch *n* passe plat *(m)*
service road *n* voie *(f)* d'accès
serviced (to be ~) *v* (appliance) être révisée
set *n* (of tools, keys etc.) jeu *(m)*
set (to) *v* (concrete, mixture) prendre; secher
set square *n* (Instrument) équerre *(f)*
set up (to) *v* (establish trade) créer
settee *n* canapé *(m)*
settle *n* (furniture) banquette *(f)* coffre
settle (to) *v* (become established) installer; (pay) payer; (pay account) régler

Sewage   **Shocking pink**

sewage *n* eaux *(fpl)* usées
sewage disposal *n* évacuation *(f)* des eaux usées
sewage outlet *n* émissaire *(m)* d'évacuation
sewage system *n* réseau *(m)* d'égout
sewer *n* égout *(m)*
shack *n* cabane *(f)*
shackle *n* fer *(m)*
shade *n* (shadow) ombre *(f);* (of colour) ton *(m)*
shaded *adj* (by trees, awning) ombragé
shadow *n* (of object) ombre *(f)*
shaft *n* (of tool) manche *(m)*
shaft *n* (e.g. power ~) axe *(m)*
shaft *n* (vent) puits *(m)*
shared ownership *n* copropriété *(f)*
sharp *adj* (chisel, knife) tranchant
sharpen (to) *v* aiguiser
sharpener *n* (occupation) aiguiseur *(m);* affûteur *(m);* rémouleur (euse) *(m)/(f)*
shatterproof glass *n* verre *(m)* de sécurité
shave (to) *v* (with plane) raboter
shave hook *n* (triangular scraper) grattoir *(m)* à fissures triangulaire
shaver point *n* (elec. socket) prise *(f)* pour rasoir électrique
shears *npl* **(garden ~)** cisaille *(f)*
shed *n* **(garden ~)** remise *(f);* **a**ppentis *(m)*
sheet *n* (plastic) feuille *(f);* (canvas) bâche *(f);* (metal) plaque *(f);* tôle *(f)*
shelf *n* étagère *(f);* tablette *(f);* (in shop) rayon *(m)*
shelf bracket *n* console *(f)* fixe (d'étagère)
shellac varnish *n* gomme laque *(f)*
shelter *n* abri *(m)*
sheltered *adj* (position) abrité
shelving *n* étagères *(fpl);* rayonnage *(m)*
shelving system *n* (adjustable brackets) console *(f)* réglable d'étagères
shingle *n* (roofing tile) bardeau *(m)*
shock *n* (elec.) décharge *(f)* électrique
shocking pink *n/adj* (colour) rose *(m)* vif

shopping area / park *n* centre *(m)* commercial

shore up (to) *v* (wall, property) étayer

short circuit *n* (elec.) court circuit *(m)*

short circuit (to) *v* (elec.) court circuiter

shovel *n* (spade) pelle *(f);* (mechanical) pelleteuse *(f)*

shovel (to) *v* enlever à la pelle

shower *n* douche *(f)*

shower attachment *n* douchette *(f)* de lavabo

shower cabinet *n* cabine *(f)* de douche

shower tray *n* receveur *(m)* de douche

show flat *n* appartement *(m)* témoin

show house *n* maison *(f)* témoin

showroom *n* exposition *(f)*

shutter *n* volet *(m)*

(louvred ~) persienne *(f)*

(single leaf of ~) vantail (aux) *(m)*

shutter hinge *n* ferrure *(f)* de volet

shutter retaining hook *n* crémaillère *(f)*

shutter stay *n* arrêt *(m)* de volet entrebâilleur

sickle *n* faucille *(f)*

side *n* (of building, property, object) **côté** *(m)* ; (of road, lake, river) bord (m)

side elevation *n* élévation *(f)* de profil

sideboard *n* buffet *(m)*

signboard *n* panneau *(m)* d'affichage

silicone *n* silicone *(f)*

silk finish *n* (paint) peinture *(f)* satinée

silvan *adj* sylvestre

silver *n/adj* (metal, colour) argent *(m)*

sink *n* **(kitchen ~)** évier *(m)*

(bathroom ~) lavabo *(m)*

(double ~) évier *(m)* à deux bacs

sink unit *n* évier *(m)* encastre

siphon *n* (WC integrated unit) siphon *(m)* monobloc; (WC – separate components) siphon *(m)* démontable

siphon (to) *v* siphonner

sisal *n* sisal *(m)*

size *n* (dimensions) grandeur *(f);* (sealant for fresh plaster) colle *(f);*

size (to) *v* (plaster) encoller

sizeable *adj* (large object) non négligeable

skeleton key *n* passe-partout *(m)inv*

skew (on the ~) *adj* de travers

skewed *adj* de travers

skew-whiff *adj* de guingois

skip *n* (for rubbish) benne *(f)*

skirting *n* (wall-bottom trim) plinthe *(f)*

skirting board *n* plinthe *(f)*

skylight *n* lucarne *(f);* fenêtre *(f)* a tabatière

slab *n* (paving etc.) dalle *(f)*

slag *n* (burnt solid fuel) stériles *(mpl);* (from metal furnace) scories *(fpl)*

slaked lime *n* chaux *(m)* éteinte

slapdash *adj* (workmanship) fait à la va vite

slate *n* (mineral) ardoise *(f)*

slate *n* (for roofing) une ardoise *(f)*

slate blue *n/adj* (colour) bleu *(m)* ardoise

slate grey *n/adj* (colour) gris *(m)* ardoise

slatted *adj* (furniture) en lames; (blinds etc) à lamelles

sledgehammer *n* masse *(f)*

sliding door *n* porte *(f)* coulissante

sliding stay *n* (adjustable for shutter / window) coulisseau *(m)* à frein réglable

slope *n* pente *(f)*

small ad. *n* petite annonce *(f)*

smallholder *n* petit exploitant *(m)*

smallholding *n* petite exploitation *(f)*

smell *n* odeur *(f)*

(bad ~) mauvaise odeur *(f)*

smell (to) *v* sentir

smith *n* (blacksmith) maréchal ferrant *(m)*

smithy *n* forge *(f)*

smoke *n* fumée *(f)*

smoke alarm *n* détecteur *(m)* de fumée

smoke detector *n* détecteur *(m)* du fumée

soak (to) *v* (wet) tremper

soakaway *n* puisard *(m)*

soap *n* (cleaning) savon *(m)*

Socket (electric)

socket *n* prise *(f)*; prise *(f)* de courant

double ~ : prise double
earthed ~ : prise de terre
recessed ~ : prise à encastrer
surface mounted ~ : prise en appliqué
trailing, single ~ : fiche *(f)* femelle
trailing ~ : (several outlets) **:** bloc *(m)* ménager; bloc *(m)* à prises multiples

---

Socket (various)

bulb ~ : douille *(f)*
screw fitting bulb ~ : douille à vis
bayonet fitting bulb ~ : douille à baïonnette
telephone ~ : prise de téléphone
television ~ : prise de télévision

---

soda *n* (chemical) soude *(f)*
sofa *n* canapé *(m)*
soft *adj* (land, ground) meuble
soft solder *n* soudure *(f)* à l'étain
soft verge *n* accotement *(m)* non stabilisé
soft water *n* eau *(f)* douce
softwood *n* bois *(m)* tendre
soil *n* sol *(m)*; terre *(f)*
soil pipe *n* tuyau *(m)* d'écoulement
solar cell *n* pile *(f)* solaire
solar heating *n* chauffage *(m)* solaire
solar panel *n* panneau *(m)* solaire
solar power *n* énergie *(f)* solaire
solder *n* **(brazing / hard ~)** brasure *(f)*
solder *n* soudure *(f)*; soudure *(f)* à l'étain
solder (to) *v* souder
soldered joint / connector *n* raccord *(m)* à souder
soldering iron *n* fer *(m)* à souder

solicitor *n* (notary) ≈ Notaire; (term of address for Notaire) Maître *n(m)* ≈ Sir / Master
solid *n* solide *(m)*
solid fuel *n* combustible *(m)* solide
solid wood *n* (not composite) bois *(m)* massif
solution *n* (liquid mixture) solution *(f)*
solvent *n* (liquid) solvant *(m)*
solvent *adj* (e.g. cleaning fluid) dissolvant
soot *n* suie *(f)*
sound *n* (wide sea channel) détroit *(m)*
sound absorbent *adj* antibruit
sound proof *adj* (structure; window) insonorisé; (product) insonorisant
sound proof (to) *v* insonoriser
soundproofing *n* isolation *(f)* phonique; insonorisation *(f)*
south *n* sud *(m)*
south facing *adj* exposé au sud
south side *n* du côté *(m)* sud
space *n* (in gen.) espace *(m);* (in building, car, etc.) place *(f)*
space (to) *v* espacer
spade *n* (garden tool) pelle *(f)*; bêche *(f)*

Spanners – and wrenches

spanner *n* clé *(f)*

adjustable ~ : clé à molette
box ~ : clé à pipe
ring ~ : clé polygonale
socket ~ : clé à douille

wrench *n* tourne-à-gauche *(m)inv*

basin ~ : clé lavabo
chain ~ : clé à chaîne
monkey ~ : clé anglaise; clé *(f)* à molette
pipe ~ *n* serre tubes *(m)*
plumbers ~ : clé Suédoise
speed ~ : clé cliquet
Stillson ~ : clé Stillson
torque ~ : clé dynamométrique

spatula *n*   spatule *(f)*
specification *n* (for construction etc.)
spécification *(f)*
speed wrench *n*   clé *(f)* cliquet
spider *n*   araignée *(f)*
spike *n*   broche *(f)*
spirit level *n*   niveau *(m)* à bulle
splinter *n*   éclat *(m)*
split (to) *v*   refendre
split level *adj*   appartement a des demi
étages
split ring *n*   anneau *(m)* brise
spokeshave *n*   wassingue *(f)*
sponge *n*   éponge *(f)*
(natural ~) éponge naturelle
(synthetic ~) éponge synthétique
spotlight *n*   projecteur *(m)*
spot weld *n*   soudage *(m)* par points
spray (to) *v* (fluid, paint) pulvériser; (fine mist)
vaporiser
spray gun *n*   pistolet *(m)* à peinture
spray paint *n*   peinture *(f)* en aérosol
spray paint (to) *v*   peindre à l'aérosol
spring (pipe bending ~) *n*   ressort *(m)* à
cintrer
spring balance *n*   balance *(f)* à ressort
sprinkler *n* (garden) arroseur *(m);* (fire
extinguishing) diffuseur *(m)*
sprinkler system *n*   système *(m)* d'extinction
automatique
spruce *n* (tree) épicéa *(m);* (timber) bois *(m)*
d'épicéa
spruce pine *n* (timber) sapinette *(f)*
spyhole *n*   judas *(m)*
square *n* (shape) carré *(m);* (tool) équerre *(f)*
stable *n* (for horses) écurie *(f)*
stable door *n*   porte *(f)* d'écurie
stack *n* (chimney) cheminée *(f)*
stage *n* (raised area) estrade *(f)*
staging *n* (working platform) échafaudage *(m)*
stain *n* (mark) tache *(f)*

Stain   Storage heater

stain *n* (product) lasure *(f)*
stain (to) *v* tacher
stain remover *n* détachant *(m)*
stain-resistant *adj* antitaches *inv*
stained glass *n* (product) verre *(m)* coloré
stained glass window *n* vitrail (aux) *(m)*
stainless steel *n* acier *(m)* inoxydable; (fam.) inox *(m)*
stair *n* (step) marche *(f)*
stair gate *n* barrière *(f)* d'escalier
stair rod *n* tringle *(f)* d'escalier
stairs / staircase *n* escalier *(m)*
stairwell *n* cage *(f)* d'escalier
stake *n* (post, support) pieu *(m)*; piquet *(m)*; (substantial post) poteau *(m)*
stake (to) *v* (in garden) mettre un tuteur à…
standard lamp *n* lampadaire *(m)*
Stanley knife ® *n* cutter *(m)*
staple *n* (hooped nail) clou *(m)* cavalier
staple *n* (for staple gun) agrafe *(f)*
staple gun *n* agrafeuse *(f)*
steam *n* (water vapour) vapeur *(f)*
steam stripper *n* (for wallpaper) décolleuse *(f)*
steel *n* (metal) acier *(m)*
(pressed ~) acier *(m)* embouti
(stainless ~) acier *(m)* inoxydable; (fam.) inox *(m)*
steel blue *n/adj* (colour) bleu *(m)inv* acier
steel wool *n* paille *(f)* de fer
step *n* (stair) marche *(f)*
stepladder *n* escabeau (x) *(m)*
stirrup latch *n* loquet *(m)* étrier
stone *n* (mineral) pierre *(f)*
stopcock *n* robinet *(m)* d'arrêt
stop tap *n* robinet *(m)* d'arrêt
stop valve *n* vanne *(f)* d'arrêt
storage *n* (unit, space) rangement *(m)*; (for furniture) garde meubles *(m)inv*
storage heater *n* (elec.) radiateur *(m)* électrique à accumulation

storage tank *n* (fuel) réservoir *(m)*; (water) citerne *(f)*

store *n* (large shop) magasin *(m)*

store room *n* (above or below ground level) cave *(f)*

storm lantern *n* lampe tempête *(f)*

stove *n* (cooker) cuisinière *(f)*; (heater) poêle *(m)*

(wood burning ~) poêle *(m)* à bois

stovepipe *n* tuyau *(m)* de poêle

straight connector *n* manchon *(m)*

straightedge *n* règle *(f)* plate graduée

strap hinge *n* penture *(f)*

straw textured wallpaper *n* paille *(f)* sur papier peint

string *n* ficelle *(f)*

striking plate (for latch, lock) gâche *(f)*

strip *n* (of wood) lame *(f)*

strip (to) *v* (paint, varnish etc.) décaper

stripped pine *n* (timber) pin *(m)* décapé

stripper (paint ~) *n* (chemical) décapant *(m)*; (tool) racloir *(m)*

(wallpaper ~) *n* décolleuse *(f)* papiers peints; **(steam wallpaper ~)** *n* décolleuse *(f)* à vapeur

stucco *n* (material) enduit *(m)*; (rendering, exterior plasterwork) stuc *(m)*

stuff *n* (unspecified material) truc *(m)*; (thing) chose *(f)*

suburb *n* banlieue *(f)*

substantial *adj* (property, holdings of land) assez grand; (object) non négligeable

surface *n* (of wall, floor) revêtement *(m)*

Surform ® *n* (tool) rabot *(m)* Surform ®

surveyor *n* (of property) expert *(m)* en immobilier

sweep *n* **(chimney ~)** ramoneur *(m)*

sweet chestnut *n* (wood, tree) châtaignier *(m)*

swimming pool *n* piscine *(f)*

Switch

switch *n* (elec.)   interrupteur *(m);* (fam.) inter

ceiling pull ~ : commutateur *(m)* plafonnier à tirette

dimmer ~ : variateur *(m)* de lumière

in line ~ : interrupteur en ligne

on / off ~ : interrupteur marche / arrêt

trip ~ : disjoncteur *(m)*

two way ~ : interrupteur de va et vient

switch off *v* (elec.) étendre

switch on *v* (elec.) allumer

---

sycamore *n* (wood, tree) sycomore *(m)*

'T' joint   Telephone extension ...

'T'-joint n (in pipes) (all equal diam.) raccord *(m)* té égal; (various diam.) raccord *(m)* té inégal
'T'-square n   double équerre *(f)*
table n   table *(f)*
tack n (tin-tack) clou *(m);* (upholstery nail) semence *(f)*
tack (to) v (attach with tacks / nails) clouer
tack hammer n   marteau *(m)* de tapissier
tack weld n   point *(m)*
tack weld (to) v   pointer
tack welding n   pointage *(m)*
tallboy n   commode *(f)* haute

Tank

tank n (general use) réservoir *(m);*

heating oil ~ : cuve *(f);*
cold water ~ : citerne *(f);*
hot water ~ : ballon *(m);*
small ~ : bac *(m)*

---

tap n (water, gas) robinet *(m)*
(mixer ~) robinet mélangeur
(self fixing ~) robinet auto perceur
tap bracket n (wall mounting) potence *(m)* porte-robinet
tap water n   eau *(f)* de robinet
tape measure n   mètre *(m)* ruban
tarmac / Tarmac ® n   macadam *(m)*
tarnish n   ternissure *(f)*
tarnish (to) v   ternir
tarpaulin n   bâche *(f)*
teak n (wood, tree) teck *(m)*
telegraph pole n   poteau *(m)* télégraphique
telephone cable n (interior) câble *(m)* téléphonique
telephone extension cable n   **rallonge** *(f)* téléphonique
telephone extension cable plug n   fiche *(m)* male téléphonique

telephone extension cable socket *n*
fiche *(m)* femelle téléphonique
telephone line *n* ligne *(f)* de téléphone
telephone socket *n* prise *(f)* de téléphone
telephone wire *n* (mostly exterior) fil *(m)*
téléphonique
tenon *n* (e.g. 'mortise and ~ ') tenon *(m)*
tenon saw *n* scie *(f)* à dos; scie *(f)* à onglets
terminal *n* (elec.) borne *(f)*
termite *n* termite *(m)*
terrace *n* (exterior leisure area) terrasse *(f)*
terrace of houses *n* alignement *(m)* de
maisons
terraced *adj* (garden, landscape) en terrasses
terracotta *n* (material) terre *(f)* cuite
terracotta *n/adj* (colour) ocre brun *(m)*
terrazzo *n* granito *(m)*
tester *n* **(circuit ~)** (elec.) testeur *(m)* de
tension
texture *n* (of surface) texture *(f)*
thatch *n* (on roof) chaume *(m)*
thatched cottage *n* chaumière *(f)*
thatched roof *n* toit *(m)* de chaume
thatcher *n* couvreur *(m)* en chaume
spécialiste
thermocouple *n* thermocouple *(m)*
thermometer *n* thermomètre *(m)*
thermostat *n* thermostat *(m)*
thick *adj* (in dimension) épais / épaisse
thickness *n* épaisseur *(f)*
thin *adj* (not thick) mince
thin (to) *v* (paint etc.) diluer
thing *n* (object) chose *(f)*
three-pin plug *n* (elec.) pris *(f)* à trios fiches
three-ply *adj* (timber panel) contreplaqué à
trois épaisseur
tiger's eye *n* (mineral) œil-de-tigre *(m)*
tile *n* (floor, wall) carreau *(m)*
(quarry ~) carreau *(m)* de terre
(roof ~) tuile *(f);*
(ridge ~) tuile *(f)* faîtière

Tile   Timber & trees

tile (carpet ~) dalle *(f)* moquette
tile (to) *v* (on floor, wall) carreler; (on roof) poser
des tuiles
tile cutter *n* coupe carrelage *(m)*
tile spacers *npl* croisillons *(mpl)*
tiled floor / tiling *n* carrelage *(m)*
tilt and turn window *n* fenêtre *(f)* basculant
timber *n* bois *(m)*

Timber & trees

alder *n* aulne *(m)*
ash *n* frêne *(m)*
bamboo *n* bambou *(m)*
beech *n* hêtre *(m)*
birch *n* bouleau *(m)*
burr walnut *n* (timber) ronce *(f)* de noyer
cherry *n* cerisier *(m)*
chestnut *n* (timber) châtaignier *(m)*
cane *n* (material) rotin *(m)*
cork *n* (material) liège *(m)*
deal *n* (timber) bois *(m)* blanc; bois *(m)* de
sapin
ebony *n* (tree) ébénier *(m)*
ebony *n* (timber) ébène *(f)*
elm *n* orme
fir *n* sapin *(m)*
holly *n* houx *(m)*
horse chestnut *n* (tree) marronnier *(m)*
(d'Inde)
larch *n* mélèze *(m)*
lignum vitae *n* gaïac *(m)*
lime *n* tilleul *(m)*
mahogany *n* acajou *(m)*
maple *n* érable *(m)*
oak *n* chêne *(m)*
oak *n* **(dark ~)** (timber) chêne *(m)* foncé
oak *n* **(light ~)** (timber) chêne *(m)* clair
pine *n* pin *(m)*

Timber & trees (continued).

pitch-pine *n* pichpin *(m)*
poplar *n* peuplier *(m)*
ramin *n* ramin *(m)*
rosewood *n* (timber) bois *(m)* de rose
sandalwood *n* santal *(m)*
satinwood *n* (timber) bois *(m)* satiné de l'Inde
spruce *n* épicéa *(m)*
spruce pine *n* sapinette *(f)*
stripped pine *n* (timber) pin *(m)* décapé
sweet chestnut *n* (tree) châtaignier *(m)*
sycamore *n* sycomore *(m)*
teak *n* teck *(m)*
walnut *n* noyer *(m)*
whitewood *n* (wood) bois *(m)* blanc
willow *n* saule *(m)*

Of timber and trees

block board *n* latté *(m)*
chipboard *n* aggloméré *(m)*
floor board *n* (composite) latte *(f);* (planks) plancher *(fpl)*
hardboard *n* isorel *(m)*
hardwood *n* bois *(m)* dur; bois *(m)* feuillu
MDF (medium density fibreboard) *n* lamifié *(m)*
plywood *n* contreplaqué *(m)* (three / five ply etc.) trios / cinq plis etc.
softwood *n* bois *(m)* tendre
solid wood *n* (as opposed to chipboard) bois *(m)* massif

Timber beam   Timber yard

timber beam *n* poutre *(f)*
timber cladding *n* revêtement *(m)* en bois
timber connector *n* connecteur *(m)* de charpente
timber merchant *n* négociant *(m)* en bois
timber yard *n* scierie *(f)*

timber clad *adj* revêtu de bois
timbered *n* **(half ~ house)** maison *(f)* à colombage ; maison *(f)* normande
timber framed house *n* maison *(f)* à colombage
timeswitch *n* minuterie *(f)*
tin *n* (metal) étain *(m);* (container) boîte *(f)*
toilet *n* (room) toilettes *(fpl)*
toilet bowl *n* cuvette *(f)*
toilet seat *n* lunette *(f)* de WC
tombac *n* (alloy) tombac *(m);* laiton *(m)*
tool *n* outil *(m)*
tool bag *n* trousse *(f)* à outils
tool belt *n* ceinture *(f)* porte-outil
tool box *n* boîte *(f)* à outils
tool chest *n* caisse *(f)* à outils
tool kit *n* trousse *(f)* à outils
tool rack *n* porte-outils *(m)*
tool shed *n* cabane *(f)* à outils
torch *n* (flame, soldering) chalumeau *(m)*
torch / flashlight *n* lampe *(f)* de poche
torque wrench *n* clé *(f)* dynamométrique
tower *n* (building, gen.) tour *(f)*
(scafford ~) échafaudage *(m)* tour
town house *n* maison *(f)* de ville
town planning *n* urbanisme *(m)*
town and country planning *n* aménagement *(m)* du territoire
trailer *n* (towed cart) remorque *(f)*
trailing socket *n* bloc *(m)* ménager
transformer *n* transformateur *(m)*
transit van *n* camionnette *(f)*
translucent *adj* translucide
transparent *adj* transparent
trap *n* **(waste water ~)** siphon *(m)*
trapdoor *n* trappe *(f)*
tree *n* arbre *(m)*
tree covered *adj* (land) boisé
tree house *n* cabane *(f)* dans un arbre
tree stump *n* souche *(f)*
tree surgeon *n* arboriculteur *(f)*

tree trunk *n* tronc *(m)* d'arbre
trench *n* tranchée *(f)*
trench (to dig a ~) *v* creuser une tranchée
trench (to fill a ~) *v* combler une tranchée
trepan *n* (cylindrical saw) trépan *(m)*
trestle *n* tréteau *(m)*
trial *n* (trying out) essai *(m)*
trial (to) *v* (to try out) tester
triangle *n* (shape) triangle *(m)*
triangular file *n* lime *(f)* tiers-point
trickle *n* (of water) filet *(m)*
trickle (to) *v* faire couler
trimmer *n* (for hedges, shrubs) taille-haies *(m)*
trip switch *n* commutateur *(m)*
trolley *n* chariot *(m)*
trowel *n* truelle *(f)*
(pointing ~) truelle *(f)* à joints
(bricklayer's ~) truelle *(f)* de briqueteur
truck *n* (lorry) camion
truss *n* (roofing) ferme *(f)* de charpente
try (to) *v* essayer
tube *n* (pipe) tube *(m); tuyau (m); (of glue;
mastic etc.) tube *(m)*
tube (copper ~) *n* tube *(m)/* tuyau *(m)* de
cuivre
tube (plastic ~) *n* tube *(m)/* tuyau *(m)* en
plastique

Tube or Tuyau?

The two terms are largely interchangable but
in general *'tuyau'* seems to tend to refer to the
larger diameter drain and down pipes while
'tube' is more confined to the small diameter
in-the-house copper and plastic tubing.
Saying *'tube'* will probably mean that you are
understood while most anglophones will be
glad to avoid the toungue-twisting challenge
of *'tuyau'*!

Tube cutter   Two way switch

tube cutter *n*   coupe tube *(f)*
turning *n* (with a lathe)   tournage *(m)*
turntable ladder *n*   échelle *(f)* pivante
turpentine / turps *n*   térébenthine *(f)*
turquoise *n/adj* (colour) turquoise *(f)*
turret lathe *n*   tour *(m)* revolver
twist drill *n* (hand tool) chignole *(f)*
twist drill *n* (bit) foret *(m)* à spire
two-pin plug *n* (elec.) pris *(f)* à deux fiches
two-ply *adj* (timber panel) contreplaqué à double épaisseur
two-stroke *adj* (engine) à deux temps
two-way switch *n*   interrupteur *(m)* de va et vient

U-bolt   Upstairs

U-bolt *n*   boulon *(m)* étrier
unblock (to) *v*   déboucher
unbolt (to) *v* (access, door) déverrouiller
unclog (to) *v*   déboucher
undercoat *n* (paint) couche *(f)* de fond
underfelt *n* (placed under roofing slates / tiles) écran *(m)* de sous toiture
underfloor heating *n*   chauffage par le sol
underground *adj* (cable, wire) sous terre
underlay *n* **(carpet ~)** thibaude *(f)*
underpin (to) *v* (building, masonry) étayer
unglazed *adj* (window, door) sans vitres
unlatch (to) *v*   soulever le loquet de ....
unlock (to) *v*   ouvrir
unscrew (to) *v*   dévisser
unsold *adj*   invendu
unventilated *adj* (room etc) non ventilé
unwanted *adj* (material, product) superflu
upholsterer *n*   tapissier (ière) *(m)/(f)*
upholstery nail *n* (tack) semence *(f)*
upstairs *n*   haut *(m)*; à l'etage *(m)*

upstand *n* (water supply) siphon *(m)* avec tube droit
use (to) *v* (machine, tool) utiliser
useful *adj* (of assistance) utile
utility room *n* buanderie *(f)*

valuation *n* (of property) évaluation *(f)*
valve *n* soupape *(f)*
(WC flushing ~) clapet *(m)*
(anti-return ~) clapet *(m)* anti-retour
(gate ~) vanne *(f)*
van *n* (small cargo vehicle) camionnette *(f);*
(larger, box) fourgonnette *(f)*
vane *n* **(weather ~)** girouette *(f)*
vanity basin *n* vasque *(f)*
vanity unit *n* meuble *(m)* sous vasque
vaporise (to) *v* vaporiser
vaporiser *n* vaporisateur *(m)*
varnish *n* vernis *(m)*
varnish (to) *v* vernir
varnished *adj* verni
varnishing *n* vernissage *(m)*
vault *n* (roof) voûte *(f);* (underground chamber) cave *(f)*
vaulted *adj* voûté
vaulting *n* (ceiling) voûtés *(fpl)*
veined *adj* (showing grain) veiné
Velcro ® *n* Velcro ®
velvet textured wallpaper *n* papier *(m)* peint velouté
veneer *n* (surface layer) placage *(m)*
veneer saw *n* scie *(f)* à placage
ventilate (to) *v* (building; room) aérer
ventilated *adj* (building; room) aéré
ventilation *n* (building; room) aération *(f);*
ventilation *(f)*
ventilator *n* (opening; vents) aérateur *(m)*

ventilator grill *n*   cour *(f)* anglaise
vermiculite *n*   vermiculite *(f)*; **(granulated ~)**
granulé *(f)* isolant vermiculite
vice *n*   étau *(m)*
video *n*   vidéo *(f)*
video recorder *n*   magnétoscope *(m)*
view *n* (scenery)   vue *(f)*
view (to) *v* (property)   visiter
viewer *n* (of property)   visiteur (trice) *(m)/(f)*
villa *n* (large town house)   pavillon *(m)*; (holiday home) villa *(f)*
village *n* (small community)   village *(m)*
village hall *n*   salle *(f)* des fêtes
vinyl *n* (material)   vinyle *(m)*
vinyl wallpaper *n*   papier *(m)* peint vinyle
violet *n/adj* (colour)   violet (ette) *(m)/(f)*
volt *n*   volt *(m)*
voltage *n*   tension *(f)*
(high ~) haute tension
(low ~) basse tension
voltmeter *n*   voltmètre *(m)*
volume *n* (cubic space)   volume *(m)*

Volume – Conversion table

Imperial Measure (UK) - Metric

1 inch^3 (in.^{3}) = 16.38 centimetre^3 (cm.^{3})
1 foot^3 (ft.^{3}) (1728 in.^{3}) = 0.03 metre^3 (m.^{3})
1 yard^3 (27 ft.^{3}) = 0.76 m.^{3}

Metric - Imperial Measure (UK)
1 cm.^{3} = 0.061 in.^{3}
1 m.^{3} = 1.308 yd.^{3} (35.315 ft.^{3})

For liquids:

Imperial Measure (UK) - Metric

1 pint = 0.57 litres
(= 57 centilitres; = 570 millilitres / cm.^{3})
1 gallon (8 pints) = 4.56 litres

Volume – Conversion table
For liquids – continued

Metric - Imperial Measure (UK)
0.5 litres (50 centilitres) = 0.88 pints
1 litre = 1.75 pints
5 litres = 1.09 gallons (8.75 pints)

Wainscot   **Wallpaper**

wainscot (to) *v* lambrisser
wainscoting *n* lambris *(m)* de appui
walk in cupboard / wardrobe *n* penderie *(f)*
wall *n* mur *(m)*
(load bearing ~) mur *(m)* portant
(party ~) mur *(m)* mitoyen
wall (to) *v* murer
wall cladding *n* plaquette *(f)* de parement
wall covering *n* revêtement *(m)* mural
wall cupboard *n* élément *(m)* mural
wall light *n* applique *(f); applique (f)* murale
wall mounted bulb holder *n* plaque *(f)*
d'applique
wall painting *n* peinture *(f)* murale
wallboard *n* (dry lining) cloison *(f)* sèche

Wallpaper

wallpaper *n* papier *(m)* peint

lining paper *n* (wallpaper) papier d'apprêt
washable ~ : papier peint lavable
vinyl ~ : papier peint vinyle;
velvet textured ~ : papier peint velouté;
fabric textured ~ : tissu *(m)* sur papier peint;
straw textured ~ : paille *(f)* sur papier peint
cork textured ~ : liège *(m)* sur papier peint

Wallpaper adhesive

wallpaper adhesive *n* colle *(f)* à papier peint

general purpose ~ : colle universelle
heavy duty ~ : colle renforcée
vinyl ~ : colle fongicide
ready mixed ~ : colle prêt à l'emploi

---

wallpaper seam roller *n* roulette *(f)* colleur ébonite
wallpaper stripper *n* décolleuse *(f)* de papier peint
(steam ~) *n* décolleuse *(f)* à vapeur
wallpaper trimming tool *n* lame *(f)* d'arasement
wallpaper trimming wheel *n* roulette *(f)* d'arasement
wall plug *n* cheville *(m);*
wall plug *n* **(expanding ~)** cheville *(m)* à expansion
walnut *n* (wood, tree) noyer *(m)*
wardrobe *n* armoire *(f)*
(built in ~) armoire *(f)* encastrée
(walk in ~) penderie *(f)*
warehouse *n* entrepôt *(m)*
warm front *n* front *(m)* chaud
warning *n* avertissement *(m)*
warped *adj* déformé
wash basin *n* lavabo *(m)*
wash basin outlet connector *n* raccord *(m)* sortie lavabo
wash leather *n* peau *(f)* de chamois
washable *adj* lavable
washable wallpaper *n* papier *(m)* peint lavable
washer *n* (metal, for bolts etc.) rondelle *(f)*
(cup ~) rondelle *(f)* cuvette
(split ~) rondelle *(f)* Grower
(tap ~ / pipe connector ~) joint *(m)*

washer-dryer *n* lave-linge / sèche-linge *(m)*
washing line *n* corde *(f)* à linge
washing machine *n* machine *(f)* à laver
washing machine drain hose *n* canne *(f)* de vidange
washing machine waste outlet *n* prise *(m)* de vidange
wasp *n* guêpe *(f)*
waste disposal *n* traitement *(m)* des déchets
waste disposal unit *n* broyeur *(m)* d'ordures
waste outlet *n* (washing machines) prise *(m)* de vidange
waste pipe *n* tuyau *(m)* de vidange; (flexible) raccord *(m)* d'évacuation souple
waste pipe connector *n* raccord *(m)* tuyau de vidange
waste pipework *n* canalisations *(fpl)* d'évacuation
waste trap *n* siphon *(m)*

Water

water *n* eau *(f)*

(drinking ~) eau *(f)* potable
(hard ~) eau dur
(mains ~) eau *(f)* de la ville
(soft ~) eau douce

---

water authority *n* compagnie *(f)* des eaux
water butt *n* citerne *(f)*
water course *n* cours *(m)* d'eau
water diviner *n* sourcier (ière) *(m)/(f)*; sourcier (ière) *(m)/(f)* radiesthésiste
water filter *n* filtre *(m)* à eau
water heater / boiler *n* chauffe-eau *(m)*
water meter *n* compteur *(m)* d'eau
water mill *n* moulin *(m)* à eau
water repellent *adj* hydrofuge
water repellent *v* (to make s'thng ~) hydrofuger

water softener *n* (device) adoucisseur *(m)* d'eau

water supply *n*   alimentation *(f)* en eau

water system *n*   système *(m)* d'alimentation en eau

water trough *n*   abreuvoir *(m)*

water wheel *n*   roue *(f)* hydraulique

waterlogged *adj* (land) détrempé

waterlogged *adj* (material e.g. carpet) plein d'eau

waterproof *adj* (material) imperméable

waterproof glue / adhesive *n*   colle *(f)* imperméable

watertight *adj* étanche

watertight (to) *v* (to make s'thng ~) étancher

watertight bar *n* (at base of door) barre *(f)* de étanchéité

waterworks *n* (for water treatment) centrale *(m)* de traitement d'eau

watt *n* (elec.) watt *(m)*

wattage *n* (elec.) puissance *(f)*

wattmeter *n* (elec.) wattmètre *(m)*

weather vane *n*   girouette *(f)*

weather strip *n* (draught / rain proofing) bourrelet *(m)*

weather strip (to) *v* mettre du bourrelet

wedge *n* (of wood, metal etc.) cale *(f)*

wedge (to) *v* caler

weevil *n*   charançon *(m)*

weight *n*   poids *(m)inv*

Weight – Conversion table

Imperial Measure (UK) - Metric

1 ounce (oz.) = 28.35 gram. (gm.).
1 pound (lb.) (16 oz.)
= 453.60 gm. {0.453 kilogram (kg.)}.
1 hundredweight (cwt.) (112 lbs.)
= 50.80 kg..
1 ton (20 cwt.)

Weight – Conversion table

Metric - Imperial Measure (UK)

1 gram (gm.) = 0.35 ounce (oz.).
100 gms. = 0.22 pounds (lbs.).
500 gms. {0.5 kilogram (kg.)} = 1.10 lbs..
1 kg. = 2.20 lbs..
100 kgs.
= 1.96 hundredweight (cwt.) (220 lbs.).
1 Metric ton (1,000 kgs.)
= 0.98 tons (19.68 cwt.).

Weighbridge   **Wheel**

weighbridge *n* pont-bascule *(m)*
weld (to) *v* souder
welding *n* soudage *(m)*
welding apron *n* tablier *(m)* de soudeur
welding gas regulator *n* (single gauge)
détendeur *(m)* à un manomètre; (twin gauge)
détendeur *(m)* à deux manomètre
welding gauntlets *n* gants *(mpl)* spécial
soudure
welding goggles *n* lunettes *(f)* de protection;
lunettes *(f)* de soudage
welding kit (arc ~) *n* poste *(f)* à souder à
l'arc
(gas ~) poste *(f)* à souder à la flamme
welding mask *n* masque *(m)* de protection
welding torch *n* chalumeau *(m)*
well *n* (pit for water) puits *(m)*
west *n* ouest *(m)*
west facing *adj* exposé à l'ouest
west side *n* du côté *(m)* ouest
wet *adj* (paint) humide; (cement, putty etc) frais /
fraîche *(m)/(f)*; (damp wall, floor) mouillé
wet rot *n* pourriture *(f)* humide; carie *(f)*
aqueuse
wet stone *n* pierre *(f)* à aiguiser
wetting agent *n* mouillant *(m)*
wheel *n* (for vehicle) roué *(f);* (smaller)
roulette *(f)*

wheel (to) *v* (barrow, cart) pousser
wheelbarrow *n* brouette *(f)*
wheely bin *n* poubelle *(f)* à roulettes
where is...... / **where are....** (please ~) SVP
(si vous plait) où est.... / où sont....
whetstone *n* pierre *(f)* à aiguiser
white *n/adj* (colour) blanc *(m)*
white goods *npl* (kitchen appliances etc.) gros
électroménager *(m)*
white hot *adj* (for metalwork) chauffé à blanc
white lead *n* blanc *(m)* de céruse
white metal *n* métal *(m)* blanc
white meter *n* compteur *(m)* 'heurs creuses'
white spirit *n* white spirit *(m)*
whitewash *n* (for buildings) lait *(m)* de chaux
whitewash (to) *v* (buildings) blanchir à la
chaux; chauler
whitewood *n* bois *(m)* blanc
wholesale *n* vente *(f)* en gros
wholesale price *n* prix *(m)* de gros
wholesaler *n* marchand (e) *(m)/(f)* en gros
width *n* largeur *(f)*
willow *n* (wood, tree) saule *(m)*
winch *n* treuil *(m)*
wind *n* (weather) vent *(m)*
windmill *n* moulin *(m)* à vent

Window

window *n* (domestic) fenêtre *(f)*

bay ~ : bow window *(m);* oriel *(m)*
casement ~ : fenêtre à battants
centre hung window ~ : (vertical) fenêtre pivotante; (horizontal) fenêtre basculante
dormer ~ : lucarne *(f)*
French ~ : porte fenêtre
roof ~ : fenêtre de toit; lucarne *(f);*
sash ~ : fenêtre à guillotine
shop / display area ~ : vitrine *(f)*
skylight ~ : lucarne *(f);* fenêtre a tabatière
tilt and turn ~ : fenêtre basculante

---

window blind *n* store *(m)*
window box *n* jardinière *(f)* à fleurs
window box *n* bac *(m)* à fleurs
window catch *n* crémone *(f)*
window cleaner *n* (occupation) laveur (euse) *(m)/(f)* de carreaux
window cleaner *n* (chemical) produit *(m)* pour nettoyer des vitres
window frame *n* châssis *(m)* de fenêtre
window glass *n* verre *(m)* à vitres
window ledge *n* appui *(m)* de fenêtre
window pane *n* vitre *(f);* carreau *(m)*
window seat *n* (domestic) banquette *(f)*
windowsill *n* appui *(m)* de fenêtre; rebord *(m)* de fenêtre
wind power *n* énergie *(f)* éolienne
windproof *adj* protège du vent (qui)
wing nut *n* écrou *(m)* à oreilles

Wire

wire *n* (thread of metal) fil *(m)*
electric ~ : fil *(m)* électrique
bell ~ : câble *(m)* paire parallèle;
copper ~ : fil *(m)* de cuivre
earth ~ : fil *(m)* d terre
live ~ : (elec. polarity) fil *(m)* de phase
neutral ~ : (elec. polarity) fil *(m)* de neutre
telephone ~ : fil *(m)* téléphonique

---

wire (to) *v* (lamp, plug) connecter; (house) installer l'électricité dans une maison
wire brush *n* (hand held) brosse *(f)* métallique; (rotary for power tool) brosse *(f)* à décaper
wire cloth *n* toile *(f)* métallique
wire cutters *npl* cisailles *(fpl)*
wire gauge *n* calibreur *(m)* à fil métallique
wire gauze *n* toile *(f)* métallique
wire mesh *n* treilles *(m)* métallique
wire nail *n* (oval ~) clou *(m)* tête d'homme; (round ~) clou *(m)* à tête plat
wire netting *n* grillage *(m)*
wire strippers *npl* (elec.) pince *(f)* à dénuder
wire wool *n* paille *(f)* de fer
wired glass *n* verre *(m)* armé
wiring *n* (in buildings) câblage *(m);* installation *(f)* électrique
wood *n* (timber, area of trees) bois *(m)*
wood *n* **(planed ~)** bois *(m)* raboté
wood glue *n* colle *(f)* bois
wood plane *n* rabot *(m)*
wood trim *n* boiserie *(f)*
wood-block *n* (flooring material) latte *(f)*
wood-block floor *n* parquet *(m)*
wood burning stove *n* poêle *(m)* à bois
wooden *adj* (made of wood) en bois
woodland *n* bois *(m)*
wood lark *n* alouette *(f)* des bois
woodlouse *n* cloporte *(m)*
woodpile *n* tas *(m)* de bois

woodscrew *n* vis *(f)* à bois
woodshed *n* remise *(f)* à bois
woodwork *n* (timber fittings) boiseries *(fpl)*
woodworm *n* ver *(m)* à bois
woodworm ridden *adj* vermoulu
working *n* marche *(f)*
(in ~ order) en état de marche
(it is not ~) il / elle ne marche pas
work surface *n* plan *(m)* de travail
work table *n* table *(m)* de travail
work top *n* plan *(m)* de travail
workbench *n* établi *(m)*
workman (woman) *n* (gen. worker / hard worker)
travailleur (euse) *(m)/(f)*; (unskilled worker)
manœuvre *(m)*;
workshop *n* atelier *(m)*
wormhole *n* (furniture, timber) vermoulure *(f)*
wrecking bar *n* (tool) pince *(f)* à décoffrer;
pince *(f)* à levier

Wrenches – and spanners

wrench *n* tourne à gauche *(m)inv*

basin ~ : clé *(f)* lavabo
chain ~ : clé *(f)* à chaîne
monkey ~ : clé *(f)* anglaise;
pipe ~ : serre tubes *(m)*
plumbers ~ : clé *(f)* Suédoise
speed ~ : clé *(f)* cliquet
Stillson ~ : clé *(f)* Stillson
torque ~ : clé *(f)* dynamométrique

Spanners

spanner *n* clé *(f)*
adjustable ~ : clé *(f)* à molette
box ~ : clé *(f)* à pipe
ring ~ : clé *(f)* polygonale
socket ~ : clé *(f)* à douille

---

wrought iron *n* fer *(m)* forge
wrought iron work *n* ferronnerie *(f)*

Xylophagous insects

xylophagous insects *npl* (wood eating / boring insects) insectes *(mpl)* xylophages

Yale   Yellow Pages

Yale ® key *n* clé *(f)* de sûreté
Yale ® lock *n* serrure *(f)* de sûreté
yard *n* (Imperial measure) Metric = 0.9144m
yard *n* (enclosed area) cour *(f)*
yardstick *n* point *(m)* de référence
yellow *n/adj* (colour) jaune *(m)*
yellow ochre *n/adj* (colour) jaune d'ocre *(m)*
Yellow Pages ® *npl* pages *(fpl)* jaunes ®

Zinc

zinc (metal) *n* zinc *(m)*

l'Auberge
sur Vézère

We offer the rare combination of a warm Welsh welcome and excellent traditional French cuisine in the heart of Corrèze, in the South West of France. The Auberge is located in the scenic village of Saint Viance, only minutes away from Rugby-famous Brive, the must-visit Dordogne valley and conveniently close to the motorways. Enjoy generous portions of good food made with finest quality regional produce in the shade of the magnificent centenary trees or in the intimate and tastefully-decorated dining room and a refreshing night's sleep in one of the peaceful en-suite rooms all with bathroom, television and direct dial overlooking the wonderfully green countryside.

Sara and Francis Debrach

L'Auberge sur Vézère
Le Bourg
19240 SAINT VIANCE
Tél : +33 (0)5 55 84 28 23
Fax : +33 (0)5 55 84 42 47

www.aubergesurvezere.com

e-mail: aubergesurvezere@wanadoo.fr

Please mention Will's DIY Dictionary
if contacting this establishment.

Opening a bank account in France is easy with CA Britline.

No need to come to France to open your French bank account as this process can be done by post.

No need to worry about having to speak to your bank in French as all of our staff are English speaking. We appreciate that it is important for you to be able to discuss your financial matters in your own language.

We offer a full range of banking services which you can apply for from the comfort of your own home.

To open an account you need to be:

resident in the UK, Ireland or France.
an existing or future French property owner or regular visitor to France.

CREDIT AGRICOLE BRITLINE
15 esplanade Brillaud de Laujardière
14050 CAEN CEDEX
FRANCE

Tel : 00.33.(0)2.31.55.67.89
Fax : 00.33.(0)2.31.55.63.99

www.britline.com

Please mention Will's DIY Dictionary
if contacting this establishment.

WELCOME (BIENVENUE) TO:
s'PASS-IMMO

If you wish to invest in a French property we have the solution for you. Our Agencies with their compliment of bilingual staff can guide you through all the necessary procedures from the initial viewing to final act .

We can help in the increasingly popular Deux-Sevres and Vendee Departments of Western France. Our Agencies are ideally located in town centres with good access to Motorway links, Ports and several Airports serving the area.

This particular area of France has retained its charm and authenticity, not to mention value for money, property prices are on the increase but remain very affordable in comparison to the rest of France.

Espass Immo (Sarl)
2 pl Donjon - 79200 Parthenay. France
Phone : 0033(0)5 49 64 00 72 (French)
Phone : 0033(0)5 49 64 56 34 (English)
www.buypropertyinfrance.com
e-mail: info@buyproperyinfrance.com

Parlons-en-Provence

FRENCH COURSES AT FAMILY-RUN CENTRE.

Parlons-en-Provence is a family run centre for adults wishing to improve their French. We are situated between Avignon and St Rémy in the heart of Prevence. Our courses are residential and are held in a secure and relaxing atmosphere,

You will be immersed in French all day, but in an enjoyable and interesting way. Whether you are studying for pleasure or to integrate into French life, our programme offers an excellent opportunity to improve your practical use of the French language.

The cuisine of Provence is world famous and during your stay with us you will be able to try authentic home cooking and sample the local wine. The visits and mealtimes are opportunities to experience Provençal life and to practice what you learn in a relaxing atmosphere.

If you have any questions or would like to make a reservation please contact us:

www.parlons-en-provence.com

E-mail: info@parlons-en-provence.com
Telephone 0033 (0)4 90 94 43 87

Please mention Will's DIY Dictionary
if contacting this establishment.

abandon *n(m)*   dereliction
abat-jour *n(m)*   lampshade
abattant *n(m)*   flap in surface, on table
abattre *v*   to knock down, pull down   (building, property)
abrasif *n(m)*   abrasive
abreuvoir *n(m)*   water trough
abri *n(m)*   shelter
abrité *adj*   sheltered (position)
abuter *v*   **to** butt (joint, pieces of wood)
acajou *n(m)adj*   mahogany (wood, tree, colour)
accélérateur *n(m)*   accelerator (adhesives etc.)
accessoires *n(mpl)* **de bain** bathroom fittings
accident *n(m)*   accident
accotement *n(m)* **non stabilisé**   soft verge
accrocher *v*   to hook (attach)
acétone *n(f)*   acetone
acétylène *n(m)*   acetylene
achat *n(m)*   purchase (something bought)
acheter *v*   to purchase
acheteur (euse) *n(m)/(f)*   purchaser
acide *n(m)*   acid
acier *n(m)*   steel (metal)
acier *n(m)* **embouti**   pressed steel
acier *n(m)* **inoxydable**   stainless steel
acre *n(f)*   acre (area of land)   metric equivalent = 0.405 ha ≈ half hectare
acrylique *n(m)*   acrylic
adaptateur *n(m)*   adapter (elec. connector)
additif *n(m)*   additive
adhérence *n(f)*   bond
adhérer *v*   to adhere
adhésif *n(m)*   adhesive
adoucisseur *n(m)* **d'eau**   water softener (device)
aérateur *n(m)*   ventilator (opening; vents)
aération *n(f)*   ventilation (building; room)
aéré *adj*   ventilated (building; room)
aérer *v*   *to* ventilate (building; room)
afficher *v*   to post (display notice etc)
affûtage *n(m)*   sharprning, grinding

Affûter   Aligner

affûter *v* to grind
affûteur *n(m)* knife sharpener (occupation)
agence *n(f)* office, branch office
agence *n(f)* **immobilière** estate agency
agence *n(f)* **de location** hire company
agent *n(m)* **immobilier** estate agent; house agent; real estate agent
aggloméré *n(m)* chipboard
agitateur *n(m)* agitator
agrafe *n(f)* staple (for staple gun)
agrafeuse *n(f)* staple gun
agrandir *v* to enlarge; to expand (room etc.)
agrandissement *n(m)* extension (of property)
agrégat *n(m)* aggregate
aide *n(f)* aid; help (general)
aide à .... aid to ....
aiguiser *v* to hone; to sharpen
aiguiseur *n(m)* knife sharpener (person)
aiguisoir *n(m)* knife sharpener (device)
aimant *n(m)* magnet
aimanté *adj* magnetic
air *n(m)* **conditionné** air conditioning
aire *n(f)* area (of place, item)
aire *n(f)* **de stationnement** parking area / apron
ajutage *n(m)* nozzle (pipe; tool)
alarme *n(f)* alarm
alarme *n(f)* **contre le vol** burglar alarm
alarme *n(f)* **contre le feu** fire alarm
alarme *n(f)* **incendie** fire alarm
albâtre *n(m)* alabaster
alcali *n(m)* alkali
alcalin *adj* alkaline
alcalinité *n(f)* alkalinity
alcool *n(m)* **à brûler** methylated spirit
alcôve *n(f)* alcove
alène *n(f)* awl; punch (hand tool for leather)
algicide *n(m)* algaecide
alignement *n(m)* **de maisons** terrace (of houses)
aligner *v* to line up

alimentation *n(f)* **en électricité** electricity supply
alimentation *n(f)* **de secteur** power supply
alimentation *n(f)* **en eau** water supply
allume feu *n(m)* firelighter
allumer *v* switch on (elec.); light (fire)
allumette *n(f)* match (fire lighting)
allumettes (une boîte d' ~) matches (a box of…)
alouette *n(f)* **des bois** wood lark
aluminium *n(m)* aluminium
ambulance *n(f)* ambulance
âme *n(f)* core (of cable)
aménagement *n(m)* development (of site)
aménagement *n(m)* **de grenier** loft conversion (planning, in progress)
aménagement *n(m)* **du territoire** town and country planning
aménager *v* to develop
amiante *n(m)* asbestos
ammoniac *n(f)* ammonia
ammoniaqué (e) *adj* ammonia-based
ampère *n(m)* ampere; amp.
ampère heure *n(m)* ampere hour
amplificateur *n(m)* amplifier
amplification *n(f)* amplification

Ampoule

ampoule *n(f)* light bulb;
~ à vis light bulb (screw cap)
~ culot 'B' light bulb (bayonet cap)
~ culot 'E' light bulb (Edison screw cap)
~ économie d'énergie energy saving light bulb
~ incandescente incandescent light bulb
néon *n(m)* neon (light)
tube *n(m)* **fluorescente** fluorescent tube

---

analyse *n(f)* analysis

analyser *v* analyse (to)
analyste *n(m)/(f)* analyst
angle *n(m)* angle
angle *n(m)* **droit** right angle
angles *adj* **(plein d'~)** angular (architecture)
anneau *n(m)* ring (circular object)
anneau *n(m)* **brise** split ring
annonce (petite ~) *n(f)* small ad.
anode *n(f)* anode
antenne *n(f)* aerial, antenna
antenne *n(f)* **parabolique** satellite aerial;
satellite dish
anthrène *n(m)* carpet beetle
antibruit *adj* sound absorbent
anti-humidité *adj* anti-humidity
antimousse *adj* **(traitement ~)** anti moss
treatment
antirouille *adj* anti-rust
antitaches *adj(inv)* stain-resistant
aplanir *v* **(s'~)** to level out (land)
appareil *n(m)* **de chauffage à gaz** gas fire
appareil *n(m)* **de mesure** gauge (gen.)
appartement *n(m)* flat
appartement *n(m)* **a des demi-étages** split
level flat
appartement *n(m)* **témoin** show flat
appeler *v* to dial ('call' a person, place)
appentis *n(m)* garden shed
appentis *n(m)* **(en ~)** lean to (hut, garage,
shed)
applique *n(f)* wall light
applique *n(f)* **murale** wall light
apprêt *n(m)* primer / size (for wood / plaster)
approximation *n(f)* approximation
appui *n(m)* **(de fenêtre)** windowsill, window
ledge
araignée *n(f)* spider
arboriculteur *n(f)* tree surgeon
arbre *n(m)* tree
arche *n(f)* arch (archway)
architecte *n(m)* architect

Architectre paysagiste   Assuré

architecte *n(m)/(f)* **paysagiste** landscape architect

architrave *n(f)* architrave

ardoise *n(f)* slate (mineral)

ardoise *n(f)* **(une ~)** slate (for roofing)

argent *n(m)adj* (metal, colour) silver; (currency) money

argile *n(f)* clay

armature *n(f)* reinforcement (in buildings, concrete)

armoire *n(f)* wardrobe

armoire *n(f)* **encastrée** built-in wardrobe

armoire *n(f)* **de toilette** bathroom cabinet

armoire *n(f)* **à linge** linen cupboard

arrêt *n(m)* **du cour** cardiac arrest

arrêt *n(m)* **d'urgence** emergency stop

arrêt *n(m)* **de volet entrebâilleur** shutter stay

arrière cour *n(f)* backyard

arrière cuisine *n(f)* scullery, back kitchen

arrimer *v* to anchor (awning; roof)

arrondi *n(m)* **(bord ~)** nosing (stair tread edge)

arroseur *n(m)* sprinkler (garden)

art *n(m)* craft (artist etc)

articulé *adj* hinged (component)

artisan (e) *n(m)/(f)* craftsman / woman (manual skills)

artiste *n(mf)* craftsman / woman (artistic skills)

asbestose *n(m)* asbestosis

ascenseur *n(m)* lift

assainissement *n(m)* waste water sanitation

assemblage *n(m)* joint (woodwork)

assemblage *n(m)* **à queue d'aronde** dovetail joint

assemblage *n(m)* **à onglet** mitre joint

assemblage *n(m)* **à tenon et mortaise** mortise and tenon joint

assembler *v* **to** assemble

assez grand *adj* substantial (property, holdings of land)

assurance *n(f)* insurance (gen.)

assuré *adj* insured

Assure   Azur

assurer *v* **(faire ~)** **to** insure
assureur *n(m)*   insurer
astiquer *v*   **to** polish (metal, glass)
atelier *n(m)*   workshop
âtre *n(m)*   grate (hearth); (hearthstone)
attenant *adj*   adjoining (building)
au dessus *adv*   overhead (above head level)
aulne *(m)*   alder (wood, tree)
auto-collant *adj*   self-adhesive
auvent *n(m)*   awning (house, restaurant)
avancée *n(f)*   overhang (of eaves)
avant-toit *n(mpl)*   eaves
avertissement *n(m)*   warning
avis *n(m)*   advice, opinion
avis *n(m)* **d'expédition**   advice note
avis *n(m)* **de réception**   advice of delivery
avocat (e) *n(m)/(f)*   lawyer
avocat (consulter un / une ~) **to seek legal advice**
axe *n(m)*   shaft (e.g. power ~)
azur *(m)*   azure (colour)

bac *n(m)*   tank (small); container
bac *n(m)* **à peinture**   paint tray
bac *n (m)* **à sable**   sandpit (garden)
bac *n(m)* **à fleurs**   window box
bâche *n(f)*   tarpaulin, sheet (canvas)
badigeon *n(m)*   lime wash
bague *n(f)*   collar (on pipework)
bague *n(f)* **de serrage**   jubilee clip
baguette *n(f)*   beading (wood or plastic strips);
conduit (general)
baguette *n(f)* **de sourcier**   divining rod
baguette *n(f)* **de plomb**   lead (for windows)
baigner *v*   to bath
baignoire *n(f)*   bath (sanitary equipment);
bathtub
bail *n(m)*   lease; let (contract)
bailleur (eresse) *n(m)/(f)*   lessor (person
granting lease)
bain *n(m)*   bath (water; chemical)
bain *n(m)* **bouillonnant**   Jacuzzi ®
baisser *v*   to lower
Bakélite ® *n(f)*   Bakelite ®
balai *n(m)*   brush (broom)
balai *n(m)* **mécanique**   carpet sweeper
balance *n(f)*   weighing scales, bathroom
scales
balance *n(f)* **à fléau**   beam balance
balance *n(f)* **à ressort**   spring balance
balayette *n(f)*   hand sweeping brush
balcon *n(m)*   balcony
ballon *n(m)* **d'eau chaude**   hot water cylinder
balustrade *n(f)*   balustrade; balcony rail
bambou *n(m)*   bamboo (plant, wood)
bande *n(f)* **élastique**   elastic / rubber band
banlieue *n(f)*   suburb
banlieue *n(f)* **vert**   garden suburb
banquette *n(f)*   bench seat; window seat
banquette *n(f)* **coffre**   settle (furniture)
barbes *adj*   barbed (spikes, thorns)
bardeau *n(m)*   shingle (roofing tile)
barillet *n(m)*   cylinder lock

barre *n(f)*   bar (strip of metal / wood)
barre *n(f)* **à rideaux**   curtain rod
barre *n(f)* **en métal**   metal bar
barre *n(f)* **de étanchéité**   watertight bar (at base of door)
barreau (x) *n(m)*   rail (fencing); rung (ladder); bar (rod of metal / wood)
barrière *n(f)*   gate (of field)
barrière *n(f)* **d'étanchéité**   damp-proof course
barrière *n(f)* **d'escalier**   stair gate
bas (basse) *adj(m)/(f)*   low
bas (en ~) *adj*   downstairs
bas *n(m)* **du porte**   excluder strip (draught; rain)
base *n(f)*   base
bas-relief *n(m)*   bas-relief
bassin *n(m)*   garden pond, fishpond, swimming pool
bâtiment *n(m)*   building (gen.); construction industry
bâtiment *n(m)* **classé**   listed building
bâton *n(m)* **de colle**   glue stick
bâton *n(m)* **de craie**   chalk (for blackboard)
batte *n(f)*   float (tool for tamping tiles)
batterie *n(f)*   battery (car, vehicles)
beaucoup *pro*   a lot (large quantity)
bêche *n(f)*   spade (garden tool); (~ à dents) garden fork
beige *n(m)adj*   beige (colour)
belvédère *n(m)*   gazebo
benne *n(f)*   skip (for rubbish)
béquille *n(f)*   ladder stay (adjustable / extending feet)
berceau *n(f)*   cradle (for baby)
béton *n(m)*   concrete
béton *n(m)* **armé**   Ferro concrete; reinforced concrete
béton *n(m)* **pré-mélangé**   ready-mix concrete
bétonner *v*   to concrete
bétonnière *n(f)*   cement mixer; concrete mixer

bidet *n(m)* bidet
biens *n(mpl)* property (buildings; land etc.);
contents of property; real estate
billes *n(fpl)* **de polystyrène** polystyrene
chips
biner *v* to hoe (ground)
binette *n(f)* hoe
biseau *n(m)* bevel
bitume *n(m)* bitumen: asphalt
blanc *n(m)adj* white (colour)
blanc (bois *n(m)* **~)** deal (timber); whitewood
blanc *n(m)* **de céruse** white lead
blanchir *v* to bleach
blanchir à la chaux *v* to lime wash;
to whitewash (buildings)
blessé *adj* injured
blesser *v* to injure
blesser (se ~) *v* to hurt (oneself)
bleu *n(m)adj* blue (colour)
bleu *n(m)* **de travail** overalls; boiler suit
(working clothes)
bleu *n(m)adj* **acier** steel blue (colour)
bleu *n(m)adj* **ardoise** slate blue (colour)
bleu *n(m)adj* **pâle** eggshell blue (colour)
bleu *n(m)adj* **pastel** powder blue (colour)
bloc *n(m)* block (slab)
bloc *n(m)* **de béton** concrete block
bloc *n(m)* **de beton cellulaire** lightweight
concrete block
bloc *n(m)* **de beton creux** hollow concrete
block
bloc *n(m)* **ménager** trailing socket (elec.)
(several outlets)
bloc *n(m)* **multiprise** multiple socket
adapter (elec.)
blocage *n(m)* jam (of machine); blockage (in
pipe gutter etc.)
blochet *n(m)* hammer beam

Bois

bois *n(m)* timber; wood; forest; woodland
~ à brûler firewood
~ dur hardwood
~ feuillu hardwood
~ massif solid wood (as opposed to re-constituted timber)
~ raboté planed wood
~ tendre softwood

Bois
Bois et arbes – Timber & trees

acajou *n(m)* mahogany
aulne *n(m)* alder
bambou *n(m)* bamboo
blanc (bois *n(m)* **~)** deal (timber); whitewood
bouleau *n(m)* birch
cerisier *n(m)* cherry
châtaignier *n(m)* chestnut (timber)
châtaignier *n(m)* sweet chestnut (tree)
chêne *n(m)* oak
chêne *n(m)* **clair** light oak (timber)
chêne *n(m)* **foncé** dark oak (timber)
ébène *n(f)* ebony (timber)
ébénier *n(m)* ebony (tree)
épicéa *n(m)* spruce
érable *n(m)* maple
frêne *n(m)* ash
gaïac *n(m)* lignum vitae
hêtre *n(m)* beech
houx *n(m)* holly
liège *n(m)* cork (material)
marronnier *n(m)* (d'Inde) horse chestnut (tree)
mélèze *n(m)* larch
noyer *n(m)* walnut
orme *n(m)* elm
peuplier *n(m)* poplar
pichpin *n(m)* pitch-pine
pin *n(m)* pine
pin *n(m)* **décapé** stripped pine (timber)

Bois et arbes –
Timber & trees (continued)

ramin *n(m)* ramin
ronce *n(f)* **de noyer** burr walnut (timber)
rose (bois *n(m)* **de ~)** rosewood (timber)
rotin *n(m)* cane (material)
santal *n(m)* sandalwood
sapin *n(m)* fir (tree)
sapin (bois *n(m)* **de ~)** deal (timber)
sapinette *n(f)* spruce pine
satiné de l'Inde (bois *n(m)* **~)** satinwood
saule *n(m)* willow
sycomore *n(m)* sycamore
teck *n(m)* teak
tilleul *n(m)* lime

Bois blanc   Boîte

bois *n(m)* **blanc** deal (timber); whitewood
bois *n(m)* **de rose** rosewood (timber)
bois *n(m)* **de sapin** deal (timber)
satiné de l'Inde (bois *n(m)* **~)** satinwood
bois (en ~) *adj* wooden (made of wood)
boisé *adj* tree covered (land)
boiserie *n(f)* wood trim
boiseries *n(fpl)* woodwork (timber fittings of house)

Boîte

boîte *n(f)* box (small); tin (container)
~ à fusibles fuse box
~ à onglets mitre box
~ à outils tool box
~ à / aux lettres letter box; post box
~ d'allumettes matchbox
~ de distribution connection box (elec.)
~ de raccordement junction box (elec.)
~ métallique canister

Boîtier de ...   Bouteille du boutane

boîtier *n(m)* **de raccordement** connector (elec. cable)

bol *n(m)* basin (bowl)

bombe *n(f)* **aérosol** aerosol (spray can)

bombe *n(f)* **de peinture** paint spray

bon *n(m)* **de commande** order form

bonde *n(f)* bunghole; plug (basin, bath etc.); plughole

bord *n(m)* bank; edge; side

bord *n(m)* **du trottoir** kerb

bord du lac *n* **(au ~)** lakeside (by the ~)

bordeaux *n(m)adj* maroon (colour)

borne *n(f)* terminal (elec.)

borne *n(f)* **de raccordement** consumer unit terminal (elec.)

bouche *n(f)* **d'égout** manhole

bouche *n(f)* **d'incendie** fire hydrant

bouche-à-bouche *n(m)* kiss of life

boucher *v* to plug (hole); to brick up (hole); to cork (bottle)

bouchon *n(m)* plug (pipe end closure); cork (bottle stopper)

boue *n(f)* mud

bougie *n(f)* candle

bougies *n(fpl)* **de ménage** household candles

boule *n(f)* ball (of clay etc); knob (on furniture, decorative)

boule (Quiès) *n(f)* ear plugs

bouleau *n(m)* birch (wood, tree)

boulon *n(m)* screw bolt

boulon *n(m)* **étrier** U-bolt

boulonner *v* to bolt (fix items together)

bourrelet *n(m)* draught excluder; weather-strip (draught-proofing)

bourrelet *v* **(mettre du ~)** to weather-strip

boussole *n(f)* magnetic compass

bouteille *n(f)* bottle

bouteille *n(f)* **du butane** butane / Calor ® gas bottle

Bouteille de gaz   Bouanderie

bouteille *n(f)* **de gaz** gas cylinder (Calor ®
type)

bouton *n(m)* **de porte** door knob

bouton *n(m)* **d'arrêt d'urgence** emergency
stop button

bouton *n(m)* knob (handle)

bouton *n(m)* **poussoir** push button

bow-window *n(m)* bay window

brai *n(m)* pitch (tar)

branchement *n(m)* **de circuit** circuit branch
(elec.)

brancher *v* to plug in (elec. circuit)

branlant *adj* loose (nail, peg)

bras *n(m)(inv)* **de flotteur** float arm (for float
valve)

braser *v* to braze (hard solder)

brasure *n(f)* hard (brazing) solder

brèche *n(f)* hole (in wall)

bricolage *n(m)* DIY - Do It Yourself

bricoler dans la maison odd-job (household)

bricoles *n(fpl)* odds and ends

bricoleur *n(m)* handyman

brique *n(f)* brick

brique *n(f)* **creuse** air brick; cavity brick

brique *n(f)* **réfractaire** fire brick

briqueteur *n(m)* bricklayer

brisé *adj* broken (glass, window)

broche *n(f)* spike

bronze *n(m)* bronze (metal)

brosse *n(f)* brush (general); paintbrush

brosse *n(f)* **de tapissier** paperhanging brush

brosse *n(f)* **métallique** wire brush (hand held)

brosse *n(f)* **à décaper** wire brush (rotary - for
power tool)

brosser *v* to brush

brouette *n(f)* wheelbarrow

broyeur *n(m)* **d'ordures** refuse disposal unit

bruit *n(m)* noise

brûleur *n(m)* **à gaz** gas ring (fixed on stove)

brunir *v* to burnish

bruyant *adj* noisy (place, machine)

buanderie *n(f)* laundry room; utility room

budget *n(m)* budget; **(à petit ~)** low-budget
buffet *n(m)* sideboard, dresser
buffet *n(m)* **de cuisine** kitchen cabinet
(furniture)
bulldozer *n(m)* bulldozer; 'dozer
bulletin *n(m)* **d'informations** fact sheet
bungalow *n(m)* chalet (holiday camp)
bulot (petit ~) *n(m)* odd-job (for cash)
bureau *n(m)* office; desk
bureau *n(m)* **de recrutement** employment
agency
burette *n(f)* **d'huile** oilcan
butane *n(m)* butane
butoir *n(m)* doorstop

cabane *n(f)* cabin; hut; shack
cabane *n(f)* **à outils** tool shed
cabane *n(f)* **dans un arbre** tree house
cabine *n(f)* **de douche** shower cabinet
cabinet *n(m)* office (gen.; small); agency
(including Estate Agency e.g. Cabinet Véronique,
Agent immobilier)
câblage *n(m)* wiring (in buildings)

Câble

câble *n(m)* cable (gen.)
~ de terre earth cable (elec.)
~ paire parallèle bell-wire
~ souple flex (elec.)
~ téléphonique telephone cable
~ câble rigide cable (installation)
~ câble souple cable (domestic, extension)

---

cache-entrée *n(m)inv* escutcheon
cacher *v* to screen (hide)
cache *n(m)* **vis** cap (for screw head)

cadastre *n(m)*   land registry
cadran *n(m)*   dial
cadre *n(m)*   frame (window, picture); setting (location)
cafard *n(m)*   cockroach
cage *n(f)* **d'escalier**   stairwell
caisse *n(f)*   box (large); chest; cash desk
caisse *n(f)* **à outils**   tool chest
calcaire *n(m)*   limestone; scale (lime deposit)
cale *n(f)*   wedge (of wood, metal etc.)
cale *n(f)* **à poncer**   sanding block
caler *v*   to wedge
calfeutrage *n(m)*   draughtproofing
calfeutré *adj*   draughtproof
calfeutrer *v*   to draughtproof
calibre *n(m)* **d'épaisseur**   feeler gauge
calibreur *n(m)* **à fil métallique**   wire gauge
calicot *n(m)*   calico
calorifugeage *n(m)*   insulation (of water tank); lagging
calorifuger *v*   **to** lag (in plumbing)
cambriolage *n(m)*   burglary
cambrioler *v*   to burgle
camion *n(m)*   lorry; truck
camion *n(m)* **de déménagement**   removal van
camionnette *n(f)*   van (small); transit van
campagnard (e) *n(m)/(f)*   rustic
canalisation *n(f)* **de gaz**   gas main
canalisations *n(fpl)* **d'évacuation**   waste pipework
canapé *n(m)*   couch; settee; sofa
caniveau *n(m)*   gully (rainwater, dishwater); gutter
canne *n(f)* **de vidange**   washing machine drain hose
canton *n(m)*   canton
cantonnier *n(m)*   road lengthsman
caoutchouc *n(m)*   rubber (substance)
capacité *n(f)*   capacity
capricorne *n(m)*   capricorn beetle

Capsule   Cave

capsule *n(f)* cap (of bottle)
capuchon *n(m)* cap (cover - e.g. valve); cowl
capuchon *n(m)* **de cheminée** chimney cowl
carbone *n(m)* carbon
Carborundum ® *n(m)* Carborundum ®
carburant *n(m)* fuel (vehicles, machines)
carbure *n(m)* carbide
carbure *n(m)* **de silicium** Carborundum®
carie *n(f)* **aqueuse** wet rot
carillon *n(m)* chime (clock); chimes (doorbell)
carillon *n(m)* **de porte** door chime
carnet *n(m)* notebook (gen.)
carnet *n(m)* **de commandes** order book
carré *n(m)* square (shape); (measure of area –
e.g. 'x' mètre carré = 'x' m^2
carreau *n(m)* tile (floor, wall); window pane
carreau *n(m)* **de terre** quarry tile
carreaux *n(mpl)* **d'une fenêtre (petits ~)**
leaded lights
carrelage *n(m)* tiled floor; tiling
carrelage *n (m)* **(coupe-~)** tile cutter
carreler *v* to tile (on floor, wall)
carrière *n (f)* quarry (stone extraction)
carte *n(f)* **hypsométrique** contour map
carte *n(f)* **magnétique** key card
carton *n(m)* cardboard; case (small box)
carton *n(m)* **bitumé** roofing felt
cartouche *n(f)* cartridge; container
cartouche *n(f)* **de gaz** gas bottle (small; for
blowlamp etc.)
cas *n(m)* **d'urgence** emergency
casque *n(m)* hard hat (safety helmet); helmet
casque *n(m)* **anti-bruit** ear defenders
casque *n(m)* **de protection** safety helmet
cassant *adj* brittle (glass etc)
cassé *adj* broken (object)
casseroles *n(fpl)* pots and pans
catalogue *n(m)* catalogue
causer des dégâts à .. to cause damage to ..
cave *n(f)* cellar; store room (not necessarily
underground); vault

ceinture *n(f)* **porte-outil** tool belt
Celsius *adj* centigrade
cendre *n(f)* ash (result of burning)
centrale *n(m)* **de traitement d'eau**
waterworks (for water treatment)
centre *n(m)* **commercial** retail centre; retail
park; shopping area
centre *n(m)* **de service** service centre
céramique *n(f)* ceramic
céramique *adj (en ~)* ceramic
cerisier *n(m)* cherry (wood, trees)
chaîne *n(f)* chain
chaînette *n(f)* **de sécurité** door chain
chaise *n(f)* chair
chalet *n(m)* cabin (holiday camp); chalet
(mountain)
chaleur *n(f)* heat
chalumeau *n(m)* blowtorch; welding torch
chambre *n(f)* room
chambre *n(f)* **à coucher** bedroom
chambre *n(f)* **du fond** back room
champêtre *adj* rustic (quaint)
chanfrein *n(m)* chamfer
chanfreiner *v* to chamfer
changer *v* to alter (gen,)
chantier *n(m)* **de construction** building site
chantier *n(m)* **de ferraille** scrap yard
chanvre *n(m)* hemp (fibre)
chape *n(f)* **de nivellement** screed (levelling)
chapelet *n(m)* beading (as a decoration on a
surface)
chaperon *n(m)* coping
charançon *n(m)* weevil
charge *n(f)* load (stuff to be carried)
chargé *adj* charged (battery)
chargement *n(m)* load (contents of vehicle)
charger *v* to charge (battery)
charges *n(fpl)* **locatives** service charge
(maintenance)
chargeur *n(m)* **de batteries** battery charger
chariot *n(m)* trolley

Charnière

Chemise

charnière *n(f)* hinge (general)
charnières *adj (à ~)* hinged
charpente *n(f)* framework (timber)
charpenterie *n(f)* carpentry (heavy construction)
charpentier *n(m)* carpenter (in construction)
charrette *n(f)* **à bras** handcart
chasse-clou *n(m)* nail punch
châssis *n(m)* **de fenêtre** window frame
châtaignier *n(m)* chestnut (timber); sweet chestnut (tree)
chatière *n(f)* cat flap
chaud *adj* hot
chaudière *n(f)* boiler (heating); furnace (central heating)
chauffage *n(m)* heating
chauffage *n(m)* **d'appoint** heater (mobile)
chauffage *n(m)* **solaire** solar heating
chauffage par le sol *n* under floor heating
chauffagiste *n (m)* gas fitter; heating engineer
chauffé à blanc *adj* white-hot (for metalwork)
chauffe-eau *n(m)* hot water cylinder / heater
chauffe-eau *n(m)* **à** gaz gas heated water cylinder
chauffe-eau *n(m)* **à électrique** electric heated water cylinder
chauffeur *n (m)* **de poids lourd** lorry driver
chauler *v* to lime (land); to whitewash (buildings)
chaume *n(m)* thatch (on roof)
chaumière *n(f)* thatched cottage
chauve-souris *n(f)* bat (flying animal)
chaux *n(f)* lime (calcium)
chaux *n(m)* **éteinte** slaked lime
chef *n(m)* **d'atelier** foreman, forewoman (of workshop / light industrial unit)
chemin *n(m)* lane (rural)
cheminée *n(f)* chimney; fireplace: flue; chimney stack
chemise *n(f)* liner (of chimney)

chêne *n(m)* oak (wood, tree)
chêne *n(m)adj* **clair** light oak (timber, colour)
chêne *n(m)adj* **foncé** dark oak (timber, colour)
chercher *v* to look for
chercher du travail to seek employment
cheville *n(f)* dowel; Rawlplug ®; Rawlbolt ®;
wall plug
cheville *n(m)* **à expansion** expanding wall
plug
cheviller *v* to dowel
chevron *n(m)* rafter
chiffon *n(m)* cloth; rag
chignole *n (f)* hand twist drill
chloration *n* chlorination
chlore *n(m)* chlorine
chlorer *v* to chlorinate
chlorure *n(m)* chloride
chose *n(f)* stuff; thing (object)
cierge *n(m)* candle (church)
cigale *n (f)* anchor ring
ciment *n(m)* cement
ciment *n(m)* **prêt à l'emploi** dry mixed
cement
ciment *n(m)* **prompt** quick setting cement
cimenter *v* to cement
cintrer *v* to bend (pipes)
circuit *n(m)* circuit (elec.)
circuit *n(m)* **principal** ring main (elec.)
circulateur du chauffage central circulating
pump
cisailles *n(fpl)* garden shears; wire cutters
cisailles *n(fpl)* **à haies** hedge clippers
cisailles *n(fpl)* **de jardinier** garden shears
ciseau (x) *n(m)* chisel
ciseau (x) *n(m)* **à bois** wood chisel
ciseau (x) *n(m)* **de briqueteur** bolster;
bricklayer's chisel
ciseaux *n(mpl)* scissors
ciseaux *n(mpl)* **de décoration** decorating
scissors

ciseaux *n(mpl)* **gros travaux** heavy-duty scissors
ciseler *v* to chisel
cité *n(f)* housing estate (large)
citerne *n(f)* cistern (in attic, underground); water storage tank; cold water tank; water butt
citerne *n(f)* **à pétrole** oil drum
citron *n(m)adj(inv)* **vert** lime green (colour)
clair *adj* light (room, colour)
clapet *n(m)* cistern exit valve; WC flushing valve
clapet *n(m)* **anti-retour** anti-return valve
classé *n* **(la maison est ~)** preservation order (the house has a ~)
classeur *n(m)* **à tiroirs** filing cabinet
clavette *n(f)* **à radiateur** radiator key

Clé

(i) **clé** *n(f)* key (for lock)

(ii) **clé** *n(f)* spanner / wrench
~ Allen *n(f)* Allen key
~ à molette adjustable spanner; monkey wrench
~ à chaîne chain wrench
~ à douille socket spanner
~ à pipe box spanner
~ anglaise monkey wrench
~ cliquet speed wrench
~ de sûreté Yale ® key
~ dynamométrique torque wrench e)
~ lavabo basin wrench
~ polygonale ring spanner
~ Stillson Stillson wrench
~ Suédoise plumbers wrench

---

clé *n(f)* **de voûte** keystone
climatisation *n(f)* air conditioning

climatisé *adj* air conditioned
cloche *n(f)* bell (chiming)
cloison *n(f)* room divider
cloison *n(f)* **mobile** screen (mobile partition)
cloison *n(f)* **sèche** wallboard (dry lining)
cloporte *n(m)* woodlouse
clôture *n(f)* fence (boundary)
clôtures *n(fpl)* fencing

Clou

clou *n(m)* nail; tin-tack

~ **à béton :** masonry nail
~ **annelé :** annulated (ringed) nail
~ **à tête perdue :** brad (floor nail);
  losthead (floor nail)
~ **béton :** masonry nail
~ **cavalier :** staple (hooped nail)

Clou (continued)

~ **galvanisé :** galvanised nail
~ **pour toiture (galvanisé) :** roofing / clout
  nail (galvanised)
~ **sans tête :** brad (floor nail); losthead (floor
  nail)
~ **tête d'homme :** oval wire nail
~ **tête plat :** round wire nail
~ **torsadé :** threaded (wire) nails
~ **striés** : striated (masonary) nails
semence *n(f)* : upholstery nail; tin-tack

---

clouer *v* to nail; to tack (attach to)
cœur *n(m)* heart
coffrage *n(m)* formwork
coffre *n(m)* chest (furniture; luggage)
coffre-fort *n(m)* safe (secure box)
coin *n(m)* nook (cosy corner)

coin *n(m)* **cuisine** kitchen area

Colle

colle *n(f)* adhesive; glue

- ~ **à papier peint** wallpaper adhesive
- ~ **bois** wood adhesive / glue
- ~ **imperméable** waterproof adhesive / glue
- ~ **mastic** mastic adhesive
- ~ **néoprène** neoprene adhesive
- ~ **ni-clou ni-vis** nail-less screw-less adhesive
- ~ **silicone** silicone adhesive
- ~ **fongicide** vinyl wallpaper adhesive l)
- ~ **prêt à l'emploi** ready mixed wallpaper adhesive
- ~ **renforcée** heavy duty wallpaper adhesive
- ~ **universelle** general purpose wallpaper adhesive
- ~ **pour...** glue for...

---

coller *v* to affix; to glue
collet *n(m)* flange
collier *n(m)* hose clip
colombages *(à ~)* *adj* half-timbered
combler une tranchée *v* to fill a trench
combustible *n(m)* **solide** solid fuel
commande *n(f)* order (commission)
commander *v* to order
commerce *n(m)* shop
commerce *n(m)* **ambulant** mobile shop
commode *n(f)* chest of drawers
commode *n(f)* **haute** tallboy
commutateur *n(m)* trip switch
commutateur *n(m)* **plafonnier à tirette** ceiling pull switch
compagnie *n(f)* **des eaux** water authority
compas *n(mpl)* **à pointes sèches** dividers (drawing instrument)

compas *n(m)* **de coupe-verre** circular glass cutter

compas *n(mpl)* **d'épaisseur** callipers (measure)

composer *v* **un numéro** to dial a number

compte *n(m)* account

compteur *n(m)* meter (gas, elec. etc.)

compteur *n(m)* **à gaz** gas meter

compteur *n(m)* **d'eau** water meter

compteur *n(m)* **d'électricité** **electric meter**

compteur *n(m)* **'heurs creuses'** white meter

comptoir *n(m)* counter (service desk)

conception *n(f)* design

conception bon (de ~) good design

conception mauvais (de ~) poor design

conduit *n(m)* conduit (pipe); flue (liner)

conduit *n(m)* **d'air** air duct

conduit *n(m)* **de cheminée** chimney flue

connecter *v* to wire (lamp, plug)

connecteur *n(m)* connector (elec. wire / cable)

connecteur *n(m)* **de charpente** timber connector

conseiller (ère) *n(m)/(f)* advisor

conseils *n (mpl)* advice

conseils à propos de ... advice about ...

conseils sur ... advice on ...

console *n(f)* **fixe (d'étagère)** shelf bracket

console *n(f)* **réglable (d'étagères)** shelving system (adjustable brackets)

consolider *v* to brace (wall; structure)

constructeur (trice) *n(m)/(f)* constructor

construction *n(f)* construction

construire *v* to construct

consultant (e) *n(m)/(f)* consultant

consulter *v* to consult

consulter *v* **un / une avocat** to seek legal advice

consulter *v* to look through (instructions, dictionary)

contaminé *adj* contaminated

contenu *n(mpl)* contents (of container, bag)

contigu (uë) (être ~ à) *v* to adjoin
contraire *n(m)* opposite
contraire *n(m)* **(tout le ~)** the exact opposite
contrat *n(m)* contract
contrat *n(m)* **d'entretien** maintenance /
service contract
contremarche *n(f)* riser (staircase)
contreplaqué *adj* laminated (wood, ply)
contreplaqué à double épaisseur two-
ply (timber panel)
contreplaqué à trois épaisseur three-
ply (timber panel)
convexe *adj* convex
copra(h) *n(m)* copra
copropriété *n(f)* shared ownership
corde *n(f)* line; rope
corde *n(f)* **à linge** clothes line; washing line
corde *n(f)* **de chanvre** hemp rope
corniche *n(f)* cornice
cornière *n(f)* angle iron
correct *adj* accurate (assessment)
corrosion *n(f)* corrosion
côté *n(m)* side (of building, property, object)
coton *n(m)* cotton
couche *n(f)* coat (of paint, plaster etc.); layer
couche *n(f)* **de fond** undercoat (paint)
couche *n(f)* **de peinture brillante** gloss
coat (of paint)
couche *n(f)* **isolant** damp-proof membrane
couche *n(f)* **(sous-~) liège** cork underlay
coude *n(m)* bend (in pipe work)
coude *n(m)* **en S** S-bend (plumbing)
coude *n(m)* **en U** U-bend (plumbing)
coude (faire un ~ à…) *v* bend (to make a ~
in …) (pipe)
coulée *n(f)* casting (metal)
couler *v* to cast (in metal)
couler *v* **(faire ~)** to trickle
couleur *n(f)adj* **de bronze** bronze-coloured
couleur *n(f)adj(inv)* **rouille** rust-coloured

coulisseau *n(m)* **à frein réglable** sliding stay (adjustable - for shutter, window)
couloir *n(m)* corridor
coup *n(m)* hit (strike a blow)
coupe *n(f)* **transversale** cross-section
coupé *adj* 'off' = not functioning (water, gas)
coupe-boulons *npl (mpl)* bolt cutters
coupe-cable *n(m)* cable cutter
coupe-circuit *n(m)* circuit breaker (elec.)
couper *v* to chop; to cut
coupe-verre *n(f)* glass cutter (tool)
coupole *n(f)* cupola
cour *n(f)* courtyard; yard
cour *n(f)* **anglaise** ventilator grill
courant *n(m)* current
courant *n(m)* **alternatif** alternating current (AC) (elec.)
courant *n(m)* **continu** direct current (DC) (elec.)
courant *n(m)* **d'air** draught (cool air)
courbe *n(m)* curve; bend (in pipework or gen.)
courbe *n(f)* **hypsométrique** contour line
cours *n(m)* **d'eau** water course
court-circuit *n(m)* short-circuit (elec.)
court-circuiter *v* to short-circuit (elec.)
coût *n(m)* cost
couteau *n(m)* knife, cutter (sharp knife)
couteau *n(m)* **pliant** jack-knife
couteau-scie *n(m)* serrated knife
couverture *n(f)* cover (protective sheet); roofing (material)
couverture *v* **(faire la ~)** to roof
couverture *n(f)* **anti-feu** fire blanket
couvreur *n(m)* roofer
couvreur *n(m)* **en chaume spécialiste** roof thatcher
craie *n(f)* chalk (mineral)
craie *n(f)* **de tailleur** French chalk
cramoisi *n(m)adj* crimson (colour)
craquelé *adj* cracked
crayon *n(m)* **à papier** lead pencil

Créer   Cylindre à air comprimé

créer *v* to create (business, trade); to establish
(business, trade)

crémaillère *n(f)* shutter retaining hook;
ratchet (rack)

crémone *n(f)* window catch

créosote *n(f)* creosote

créosoter *v* to creosote

crépi *n(m)* rendering (surface layer on building);
roughcast;

crépi *adj* rendered

crépi *n(m)* **gravillonné** pebble dash

crépir *v* to render; to roughcast (wall etc,)

creuser *v* to deepen (dig out); to dig; to
excavate

creux *n(m)* groove (in screw)

cric *n(m)* jack (for lifting weights)

crise *n(f)* **cardiaque** heart attack

crochet *n(m)* hook

crochet *n(m)* **à visser** cup hook, screw hook;

crochet à visser epoxy (noir / blanc) plastic
coated (black / white) cup hook / screw hook

crochet *n(m)* **en S** butcher's hook

croisillons *n(mpl)* tile spacers

cuir *n(m)* leather

cuisine *n(f)* kitchen

cuisinière *n(f)* cooker; stove

cuisinière *n(f)* **à gaz** gas cooker

cuisinière *n(f)* **électrique** electric cooker

cuivre *n(m)adj* copper (metal / colour)

cuivre *n(m)* **jaune** brass (metal)

cuivres *n(mpl)* the brass (ornaments etc.);
copperware

cutter *n(m)* Stanley knife ®

cuve *n(f)* oil tank (domestic)

cuvette *n(f)* bowl; toilet bowl

cylindre *n(m)* cylinder (general)

cylindre *n(m)* **à air comprimé** compressed
air cylinder

dalle *n(f)* flagstone; paving stone; slab
dalle *n(f)* **moquette** carpet tile
dalles *n(fpl)* paving
débarras *n(m)* box room; junk room
débordant *adj* overflowing (bath; sink; d'bin)
déboucher *v* to unblock; to unclog
déboucheur *n(m)* drain plunger (implement)
déboucheur *n(m)* **à tiges (flexibles)** drain rods (flexible)
déboucheur *n(m)* **liquide** drain clearing fluid
décapage *n(m)* cleaning (of surfaces during building & painting works etc.)
décapant *n(m)* flux; paint remover (chemical); paint stripper (chemical)
décaper *v* to clean (surfaces during building & painting works etc.)
décaper *v* to strip (paint, varnish etc.)
décentré *adj* off-centre
décharge *n(f)* **électrique** electric shock
décharge *n(f)* **publique** rubbish dump
déchets *n(mpl)* refuse
déchets *n(mpl)* **de jardin** garden waste
déchetterie *n(f)* refuse dump
décolleuse *n(f)* tool or agent for stripping wallpaper or paint
décolleuse *n(f)* **à vapeur** steam stripper
décolleuse *n(f)* **de papier peint** wallpaper stripper
décolleuse *n(f)* **de peint** paint stripper (chemical)
décoloré *adj* faded
décombres *n(mpl)* debris
décorateur (trice) *n(m)/(f)* decorator
découpure *n(f)* fretwork
déduire *v* to deduct
défaut *n(m)* defect; fault
déformé *adj* warped
déformer *v* to contort
dégâts *n(mpl)* damage
dégâts *n(mpl)* **du feu** fire damage
degrés *n(mpl)* **Celsius** degrees centigrade

dehors *adv* outdoor
DEL *n(f)* **(diode électroluminescente)** LED
(light emitting diode)
délabré *adj* decrepit (building)
délabrement *n(m)* decay (of building; façade)
déménagement *n(m)* moving house
déménager *v* to move house
déménageur *n(m)* furniture remover
demeure *n(f)* mansion; residence
demeure *n(f)* **familiale** family dwelling
demi *adj* half; ½ (a measure)
demi-hectare *n(m)* land area of 5,000 sq. m.
= 1.24 acres (6,000 sq. yds.)
démolir *v* to demolish
démonstration *n(f)* demonstration (of
machines etc.
demonter *v* to take down; to dismantle
démontrer *v* to demonstrate (illustrate)
dentée *adj* **(à lame ~)** saw-edged blade
dépanneur *n* engineer (repair man)
dépendance *n(f)* outbuilding
déposer *v* to dump
dépôt *n(m)* depot
dépôt *n(m)* **de matériaux de construction**
builder's yard
descente *n(f)* **de gouttière** drainpipe
déshumidifier *v* to dehumidify
desserré *adj* loose (screw)
desserrer *v* to loosen (most fixtures)
dessin *n(m)* **à l'échelle** scale drawing
détachant *n(m)* stain remover
détartrant *n(m)* descaler
détartrer *v* to descale
détecteur *n(m)* sensor
détecteur *n(m)* **de fumée** smoke alarm;
smoke detector
détecteur *n(m)* **infrarouge** infrared sensor
détendeur *n(m)* **à deux manomètre** welding
gas regulator (twin gauge)
détendeur *n(m)* **à un manomètre** welding gas
regulator (single gauge)

détrempé *adj*   waterlogged (land)
détroit *n(m)*   sound (wide sea channel)
deux temps *adj* **(à ~)**   two-stroke (engine)
déverrouiller *v*   to unbolt (access, door)
devis *n(m)*   estimate (written quote)
dévisser *v*   to unscrew
dextérité *n(f)*   craftsmanship
diagonale *n(f)*   diagonal
diamant *n(m)*   diamond; glass cutter (tool)
diamètre *n(m)*   diameter
diamètre *n(m)* **externe**   external diameter
diesel *n(m)*   diesel (car, van)
diffuseur *n(m)*   sprinkler (fire extinguishing)
dilué *adj*   dilute
diluer *v*   to dilute; to thin (paint etc.)
dimension *n(f)*   measurement; dimension
diode *n(f)* **électroluminescente (DEL)**   light emitting diode (LED)
directeur (trice) *n(m)/(f)*   director (of business – job title)
diriger *v*   to control (direct)
disjoncteur *n(m)*   circuit breaker (elec.); trip switch (elec.)
disjoncteur *n(m)* **différentiel**   RCD (residual current device)
disposer *v*   to dispose (of furniture / things)
disque *n(m)* **abrasif**   sanding disc
disque *n(m)* **diamant**   diamond cutting disk
disque *n(m)* **diamant carrelage**   diamond tile-cutting disk
dissolvant *adj*   solvent (e.g. cleaning fluid)
dissoudre *v*   to dissolve (create solution)
distillation *n(f)*   distillation
distiller *v*   to distil
divan-lit *n(m)*   divan bed
dôme *n(m)*   dome
dormant *n(m)*   door frame
double vitrage *n(m)*   double glazing
douche *n(f)*   shower
douchette *n(f)* **de lavabo**   shower attachment

Douille   Durcisseur

douille *n(f)* bulb socket / holder (elec.)
douille *n(f)* **à baïonnette** bayonet bulb socket
douille *n(f)* **à vis** screw bulb socket
drain *n(m)* drain (for escaping water)
drainage *n* drainage
drainer *v* to drain (garden, standing water)
drap *n(m)* **de billard** baize
droit *adj* level (household fittings e.g. shelf)
droit *adj* **(à angle ~)** right-angled
droit *n(mpl)* **de pacage** grazing rights
droit *n(m)* **de passage** right of way (on a lane, property)
durcisseur *n(m)* **pour plâtre** primer (stabilising)

Eau   Échafaudage

Eau

eau *n(f)* water
~ calcaire hard water
~ courant mains water
~ de javel bleach
~ de la ville mains water
~ de robinet tap water
~ distillée distilled water
~ douce soft water
~ potable drinking water

---

eau *adj* **(plein d'~)** waterlogged (material - e.g. carpet)
eaux *n(fpl)* **usées** sewage
ébène *n(f)* ebony (timber); **(noir d'~)** jet
black (colour)
ébénier *n(m)* ebony (tree)
écailler *v* **(s'~)** to flake off (paint etc.)
écarlate *n(f)adj* scarlet (colour)
échafaudage *n(m)* scaffold (building);
scaffolding; staging (working platform)

échafaudage *n(m)* **tour** scaffold tower
échantillon *n(m)* sample
échapper *v* to leak (from container, tank)

Échelle

échelle *n(f)* ladder; scale (gradations)
~ **accordéon** collapsible loft ladder
~ **coulissante** extension ladder; sliding loft ladder
~ **d'accès** loft ladder
~ **escamotable** retractable loft ladder
~ **pivante** turntable ladder
~ **télescopique** extending ladder
escabeau (x) *n(m)* step ladder

éclairage *n(m)* lighting (gen.)
éclairage *n(m)* **de sécurité** security lighting
éclairer *v* to light (illuminate)
éclairs *n(mpl)* lightning
éclat *n(m)* splinter
éclater *v* to burst (pipe; boiler)
écran *n(m)* **de cheminée** fire screen
écran *n(m)* **de sous-toiture** underfelt (placed under roofing slates / tiles)
écrou *n(m)* nut (and bolt)
écrou *n(m)* **à oreilles** wing nut
écurie *n(f)* stable (for horses)
effluent *n(m)* effluent
effriter *v* **(s'~)** to flake off (plaster, cladding etc.)
égout *n(m)* sewer
égoutter *v* to drain (items after washing)
égouttoir *n(m)* draining board
électricien (ienne) *n(m)/(f)* electrician
électricité *n(f)* electricity
électricité *n(fpl)* **du secteur** electric mains
électrique *adj* electric
électrocuter *v* **(s'~)** electrocuted (to be ~) (accident)

électroménager *n(mpl)* **(gros ~)** white goods (kitchen appliances etc.)

élément *n(m)* **de cuisine** kitchen unit

élément *n(m)* **mural** wall cupboard

élévateur *n(m)* elevator (hoist)

élévation *n(f)* elevation (architectural drawing)

élévation *n(f)* **de la façade front** elevation

élévation *n(f)* **d'arrière** rear elevation

élévation *n(f)* **latérale / de profil** side elevation

éliminer *v* to exterminate (vermin)

ellipse *n(f)* ellipse

émail *n(m)* enamel

emballage *n(m)* packaging

emballer *v* to pack (place in carton etc)

embouteillage *n(m)* traffic jam

embrasure *n(f)* **de porte** doorway (frame)

émissaire *n(m)* **d'évacuation** sewage outlet

émoussé *adj* blunt (knife, chisel)

émousser *v* to blunt

employeur (euse) *n(m)/(f)* employer

encastré *adj* built-in (furniture)

enclos *n(m)* paddock

encocher *v* to notch (to mark)

encoignure *n(f)* corner cupboard

encoller *v* to paste (wallpaper etc.); to size (plaster)

endroit *n(m)* location (place, district)

enduire *v* to coat (cover with); to render (wall)

enduit *n(m)* filler (product); rendering (mortar, cement, plaster mix); stucco (exterior plaster)

enduit *n(m)* **à prise rapide** filler (quick setting)

enduit *n(m)* **d'étanchéité** sealant / sealer (coating)

énergie *n(f)* **électrique** power (elec.)

énergie *n(f)* **éolienne** wind power

énergie *n(f)* **solaire** solar power

enfaîteau *n(m)* ridge tile

enlever à la pelle *v* to shovel

enquêter sur… *v* to investigate (enquire about …)

enquêteur (trice) *n(m)/(f)* investigator (fraud, insurance)

enrouleur *n(m)* **de câble** cable reel

ensemble *n(m)* **de circuit** circuitry (elec.)

ensemble *n(m)* **d'habitation housing** development

entaille *n(f)* notch (cut in wood etc.)

entonnoir *n(m)* funnel (for pouring)

entrée *n(f)* hall (in house); entrance (point of entry); inlet (valve etc.); lobby (of house)

entrepôt *n(m)* warehouse

entrepreneur (euse) *n(m)/(f)* contractor; entrepreneur

entrepreneur *n(m)* **dans l'immobilier** house builder

entrepreneur *n(m)* **en bâtiment** builder (gen.)

entreprise *n(f)* enterprise (company); firm (business)

entreprise *n(f)* **de bâtiment** building company

entretien *n(m)* maintenance

envers *adj* **(à la ~)** inverted (upside-down);

environ *adv* approximately (about, approx.)

envoi *n(m)* **contre remboursement** COD (Cash on Delivery).

envoyé en exprès send by express

envoyer une facture à .... *v* to send an invoice to....

épais (épaisse) *adj(m)/(f)* thick (in dimension)

épaisseur *n(f)* thickness

épicéa *n(m)* spruce (wood, tree)

épingle *n(f)* pin (to attach paper, textiles)

épingle *n(f)* **de sûreté** safety pin

éponge *n(f)* sponge; **(~ naturelle)** natural sponge; **(~ synthétique)** synthetic sponge

équarri *adj* rough-hewn (stone, timber)

équerre *n(f)* angle bracket (flat); bracket (for shelf); set square (Instrument, tool); **(double ~)** T square

équerre *n(f)* **de montage** angle plate

équipement *n(m)* equipment

Équipements   Évaluation

équipements *n(mpl)* fixtures and fittings
(property deals)
équiper *v* to equip
érable *n(m)* maple (wood, tree)
érafler *v* to scrape; to scratch (make a mark)
éraflure *n(f)* scratch (mark on paintwork etc.)
escabeau (x) *n(m)* stepladder
escalier *n(m)* stairs; staircase
escalier *n(m)* **de secours** fire escape
escalier *n(mpl)* **de service** backstairs
espace *n(m)* space (available area)
espacer *v* to space (spread out)
espèces *n(fpl)* **cash**
essai *n(m)* trial (trying out)
essai *n(m)* **(à l'~)** on appro. (on approval)
essayer *v* to try
essuie-verres *n(m)* glass cloth
est *n(m)* east; **(du côté** *(m)* **~)** east side
est (exposé à l'~) *adj* east-facing
estrade *n(f)* stage (raised area)
établi *n(m)* workbench
étage *n(m)* floor (storey)
étagère *n(f)* rack (storage); shelf
étagère *n(f)* **de séparation** room divider
étagères *n(fpl)* shelving
étain *n(m)* tin (metal)
étamine *n(f)* muslin
étanche *adj* watertight
étancher *v* to watertight (to make s'thng ~)
étang *n(m)* pond; small lake
étau *n(m)* vice (tool)
étayer *v* to shore up (wall, property); to
underpin (building, masonry)
éteindre *v* to extinguish (fire)
éteint 'off' = not functioning (elec. appliances)
étendre *v* switch off (elec.)
étoupe *n(f)* oakum
étui *n(m)* case (protective box)
évacuation *n(f)* **des eaux usées** sewage
disposal
évaluation *n(f)* valuation (of property)

Évaluer   Extraire

évaluer *v* to estimate (guesstimate)
évier *n(m)* kitchen sink
évier *n(m)* **à deux bacs** double sink
évier *n(m)* **encastre** sink unit
examiner *v* to examine
excavateur *n(m)* digger; excavator
exemple *n(m)* example
expédier *v* to send (by post or carrier)
expert *n(m)* expert
expert *n(m)* **en immobilier** property surveyor
expert *n(m)* **foncier** land agent
expert *n(m)* **géomètre** building surveyor
exploitant *n(m)* **(petit ~)** smallholder
exploitation *n(f)* holding (land)
exploitation agricole *n(m)* agricultural
holding; **(petite ~)** smallholding
exposé *n(m)* **(bref ~)** outline (gen. idea)
exposer brièvement *v* **to** outline (give the
gen. idea)
exposition *n(f)* showroom
extérieur *n(m)* outside (of property)
extérieur *adv* **(à l' ~)** outdoor; outside
extincteur *n(m)* fire extinguisher
extraire *v* to quarry (extract stone etc.)

Fabricant   Fauteuil

fabricant *n(m)* manufacturer
fabriquer *v* to manufacture
façade *n(f)* façade; frontage (of house)
facture *n(f)* bill; invoice
facture *n(f)* **définitive** final invoice
faire *v* to make
faîtage *n(m)* ridge (roof)
faîte *n(m)* ridge (roof)
faner *v* to fade (loose intensity)
faucille *n(f)* hook (horticultural); sickle
fauteuil *n(m)* chair (upholstered)

fax *n(m)*   fax
faxer *v*   to fax
fêlure *n(f)*   crack (in pottery, wall etc.)

Fenêtre

fenêtre *n(f)*   window (domestic)

~ **à battants**   casement window
~ **à croisillons de plomb**   lattice window
~ **à guillotine**   sash window
~ **à petits carreaux**   leaded window
~ **a tabatière**   skylight
~ **basculante**   centre-hung window
  (horizontal); tilt and turn window
~ **de toit**   roof window
~ **fenêtre** *n(f)* **de toit**   roof window
~ **pivotante**   centre-hung window (vertical)
~ **(porte ~)**   French window

---

fente *n(f)*   groove (in screw)

Fer

fer *n(m)*   iron (metal); shackle

~ **à jointoyer**   pointing iron
~ **à repasser**   iron (smoothing ~)
~ **à souder**   soldering iron
~ **équerre**   L-iron
~ **forgé**   wrought iron

---

ferme *n(f)*   farmhouse
ferme *n(f)* **de charpente**   truss (roofing)
fermé   'off' = not functioning (tap)
ferme-porte *n(m)*   door-closer
fermer à clé *v*   to lock (with key)
fermer à double tour *v*   to double-lock
fermer au loquet *v*   to latch
fermette *n(f)*   farmhouse (small, gen. ancient)
ferraille *n(f)*   scrap iron / metal
ferreux (euse) *adj*   ferrous

ferronnerie *n(f)* wrought iron / metal work;
ferronnier (ière) *n(m)/(f)* iron craftsman /
woman
ferrure *n(fpl)* iron fittings; **(~ de porte)** door
ironwork; **(~ de volet)** shutter ironwork
ferrures *npl(fpl)* metal household fittings
feu *n(m)* fire (gen.)
feuillard *n(m)* razor wire
feuille *n(f)* sheet (plastic)
fibre *n(f)* fibre (textiles, wood)
fibre *n(f)* **artificielle** artificial fibre
fibre *n(f)* **de verre** glass fibre
fibre *n(f)* **synthétique** synthetic fibre
fibres *n(fpl)* **de verre** fibreglass
fibres irrégulières *adj* cross-grained (wood)
ficelle *n(f)* string
fiche *n(f)* plug (elec.): pin (of elec. plug)
fiche *n(f)* **femelle** socket (trailing, single)
fiche *n(m)* **femelle téléphonique** telephone
extension cable socket
fiche *n(m)* **male téléphonique** telephone
extension cable plug

Fil

fil *n(m)* lead (elec. cable); wire (thread of metal)

~ à plomb plumb line
~ de cuivre copper wire
~ de fer barbelé barbed wire
~ de neutre wire (neutral ~) (elec.)
~ de phase wire (live ~) (elec.)
~ de terre wire (earth ~) (elec.)
~ sous tension live wire (elec.)
~ téléphonique telephone wire

---

filament *n(m)* filament (elec.)
file *n(f)* line (row of people, cars)
filet *n(m)* mesh (fabric); net (general); trickle (of
water)
filtre *n(m)* **à eau** water filter

finition *n(f)*   finish (quality of appearance)
fioul *n(m)*   fuel oil
fioul *adj* **(au ~)** oil-fired (heating etc.)
fissure *n(f)*   crack (in pottery, wall etc.);
fissure (in building)
fixé *adj* placed; positioned
fixer *v*   to fix (put in place)
flamme *n(f)*   flame
fleuron *n(m)*   finial
flexible *n(m)* **d'alimentation** flexible
connector (plumbing, lengthy)
flotteur *n(m)*   float (for float valve)
foncé *adj* dark (room, paint etc)
foncer *v*   to darken
fond *n(m)*   bottom
fondant *n(m)* flux (for solder)
fondations *n(fpl)* foundations
fonderie *n(f)* foundry
fondre *v* **(faire ~)** to melt
fongique *adj* fungal
fonte *n(f)* cast iron
forcer à la pince-monseigneur *v* to jemmy
(lever)
forer *v* to drill (metal; masonry)
foret *n(m)* drill bit (metal; masonry)
foret *n(m)* **à spire** twist drill (bit)
foreuse *n(f)* auger (in land, soil)
forge *n(f)* smithy
forgeron *n(m)* blacksmith
forme de balle *adj* **(en ~)** ball shaped
formica ® *n(m)* Formica ®
fossé *n(m)* ditch
fosse *n(f)* **d'aisances** cesspit; cesspool
fosse *n(f)* **septique** septic tank; cesspit
foudre *n(f)* lightning strike
four *n(m)* oven; kiln
four *n(m)* **à chaux** lime kiln
four *n(m)* **à gaz** gas oven
fourche *n(f)* fork (garden tool); pitchfork
fourgonnette *n(f)* box van
fourmi *n(f)* ant

fourmi *n(f)* **noir (commune)** black ant
fourneau *n(m)* **(de cuisine)** range (kitchen ~)
fourneau *n(m)* **à gaz** gas range
foyer *n(m)* hearth (more figurative ≈ home)

Frais

frais *n(mpl)* expenses

frais *n(mpl)* charge (cost of service)

~ **de construction** building costs
~ **de 'Francis'** 'Francis's' expenses
~ **de déplacement** call out charge
~ **de transport** haulage charge
~ **d'entretien** maintenance fees

---

frais (fraîche) *adj* wet (cement, putty etc)
fraiser *v* to countersink (grind / drill hole)
frapper *v* to hit (strike)
frêne *n(m)* ash (wood; tree)
frise *n(f)* frieze
froid *n(m)* cold
front *n(m)* **chaud** warm front
fuir *v* to leak
fuite *n(f)* leak (in roof; tank; pipe); seepage
fuite *n(f)* **de gaz** gas leak
fumée *n(f)* smoke
fusible *n(m)* fuse (elec.)
fusible *n(m)* **à cartouche** cartridge fuse
fusible *n(m)* **principal** main fuse
fusible a sauté (un ~) a fuse has blown
fût *n(m)* cask (beer)

Gâche   ## Grain de veines

gâche *n(f)* striking plate (for latch, lock)
gaïac *n(m)* lignum vitae (wood, tree)
galvaniser *v to* galvanize
gant *n(m)* **en caoutchouc** rubber glove
gants *n(mpl)* **spécial soudure** welding gauntlets
garde-manger *n(m)* larder; pantry
garde-meubles *n(m)/(inv)* storage (for furniture)
garniture *n(f)* **de chaudière** lagging jacket
gaz *n(m)* gas
gaz *n(m)* **de haut fourneau** flue gas
gaz *n(mpl)* **de pétrole liquéfiés (GPL)** liquefied petroleum gas (LPG)
gaz *n(mpl)* **de ville** mains gas
gazer *v* **to** gas
gazole *n(m)* diesel fuel; diesel oil
gazon *n(m)* grassed area (also turf)
générateur *n(m)* generator (elec.)
genouillère *n(f)* knee-pad
gérant (e) *n(m)/(f)* manager
girouette *n(f)* weather vane
glace *n(f)* looking glass; mirror
glace *n(f)* **biseautée** bevelled mirror
glissement *n(m)* **de terrain** landslide / landslip
godet *n(m)* bucket of mechanical digger / excavator
gomme *n(f)* rubber (eraser)
gomme-laque *n(f)* shellac; shellac varnish
gond *n(m)* hinge (lift-off)
gond *n(m)* **à visser** right angle screw hook
goujon *n(m)* pin; panel pin (fine nail)
goupille *n(f)* **fendue** cotter pin
goutte *n(f)* drip
goutter *v* **to** drip
gouttière *n(f)* gutter (on eaves)
gouttières *n(fpl)* guttering
GPL *n(mpl)* **(gaz de pétrole liquéfies)** LPG (liquefied petroleum gas)
grain *n(m)* **de veines** grain (in wood)

grain fin *adj*   fine-grained (timber)
graissage *n(m)*   lubrication (engines, machines)
graisse *n(f)*   lubricant (= grease)
graisse *n* **(pompe** *(f)* **à ~)**   grease gun
grand *adj*   big
grand bassin *n(m)*   deep end
grandeur *n(f)*   size (dimensions)
grange *n(f)*   barn
granit(e) *n(m)*   granite
granito *n(m)*   terrazzo
gratté *adj*   brushed (textiles)
gratter *v*   **to** scrape (clean)
grattoir *n(m)* **à fissures triangulaire**
shave-hook (triangular scraper)
gravats *n(mpl)*   rubble (building)
gravière *n(f)*   gravel pit
graviers *n(mpl)*   gravel (coarse)
gravillonné *adj*   gravelled (drive; path; area)
gravillonner *v*   to gravel
gravillons *n(mpl)*   chippings; gravel (fine)
grenier *n(m)*   attic; granary; loft
grenier *n(m)* **aménagé**   habitable loft / attic
grès *n(m)*   sandstone
grillage *n(m)*   mesh (metal); wire netting
grille *n(fpl)*   bars (on window); grating
grille *n(f)* **de foyer**   grate (fire container)
grincer *v*   to rasp
gris *n(m)adj*   grey (colour)
gris *n(m)adj* **ardoise**   slate grey (colour)
grossir *v*   to magnify
grossiste *n(m)* **en plomberie**   plumber's
merchant
grue *n(f)*   crane
guêpe *n(f)*   wasp
guillaume *n(m)*   rabbet plane
guingois *adj* **(de ~)**   skew-whiff
gypse *n (m)*   gypsum

habitable *adj* habitable
hache *n(f)* axe
hachette *n(f)* hatchet
haie *n(f)* hedge
haut *n(m)* **(à l'étage)** upstairs
haute résistance (à) *adj* heavy-duty
haute tension *n(m)* high voltage
haute tension (à) *adj* high voltage
hauteur *n(f)* height (of object)
hectare *n(m)* (10,000 sq m) = 2.47 acres
herbe *n(f)* grass (general)
hérisson *n(m)* chimney brush
hêtre *n(m)* beech (tree; wood); **(~ pourpre)**
copper beech (tree)
heures *n(fpl)* **d'ouverture** opening hours (of
shops etc.)
heurtoir *n(m)* door knocker
hisser *v* to hoist
horizontal *adj* level (horizontal)
hors courant *adj* dead (elec. circuit)
hôtel *n(m)* **des ventes** saleroom
houe *n(f)* hoe
housse *n(f)* dust sheet
houx *n(m)* holly (wood; tree)
huile *n(f)* oil (lubricating)
huile *adj* **(à base d' ~)** oil-based (paint)
huile *n(f)* **de graissage** lubricating oil
huile *n(f)* **de lin** linseed oil
huile *n(f)* **de ricin** castor oil
humide *adj* damp (building, wall floor etc);
humid; wet (paint)
humidificateur *n(m)* humidifier
humidité *n(f)* damp; humidity; moisture
humidité *n(f)* **s'élevant du sol** rising damp
hydrofuge *adj* water repellent
hydrofuger *v* to make water repellent

idée *n(f)* outline (gen. idea)
identifier *v* to diagnose (problem)
ignifugé *adj* fireproof
ignifugeant *n(m)* flame retardant
ignifuger *v* to fireproof
immeuble *n(m)* building (house / flats / offices)
immobiliers *n(mpl)* property (buildings; land etc.); real estate
imperméable *adj* damp-proof; waterproof (material); impermeable (membrane, rock)
imputrescible *adj* rotproof
incendie *n(m)* fire (major)
incendies *n(fpl)* **(normes** *(f)* **de protection contre les ~)** fire regulations
indestructible *adj* indestructible
indicateur *n(m)* **de pression** pressure gauge
infiltration *n(f)* seepage (drainage to land / water)
inflammable *adj* flammable; inflammable; **(hautement ~)** highly flammable
inodore *adj* odourless
inondation *n(f)* flood / flooding
inonder *v* to flood (house, area)
inox *n(m)* stainless steel
inoxydable *adj* rust-proof (metal)
insectes *n(mpl)* **xylophages** xylophphagous insects (wood eating / boring)
insonorisant *adj* sound-proof (product)
insonorisation *n(f)* soundproofing
insonorisé *adj* sound-proof (structure; window)
insonoriser *v* to sound-proof
installation *n(f)* fixture (immovable thing)
installation *n(f)* **électrique** wiring (in buildings)
installer *v* to settle (become established)
installer *v* **l'électricité dans une maison** to wire a house
instructions *n(fpl)* instructions
instrument *n(m)* instrument
intégré *adj* fitted (cupboards, kitchens)
inter *n* switch (elec.) (fam.)

interphone *n(m)* entry phone; intercom
interrupteur *n(m)* switch (elec.)
interrupteur *n(m)* **différentiel** main switch
interrupteur *n(m)* **en ligne** in-line switch
(elec.)
interrupteur *n(m)* **marche - arrêt** on - off
switch (elec.)
invendu *adj* unsold
inventeur (trice) *n(m)/(f)* inventor
invention *n(f)* invention
isolant *n(m)* insulating material; lagging
isolateur *n(m)* insulator (electric)
isolation *n(fpl)* insulation
isolation *n(f)* **des murs creux** cavity wall
insulation
isolation *n(f)* **phonique** soundproofing
isolation *n(f)* **thermique** thermal insulation;
(~ en mousse) foam thermal insulation
isolé *adj* isolated
isolement *n(m)* isolation
isoler *n(m)* insulate (general)
isoler *v* to insulate; to lag (roof)
isoler contre calorifugé insulate (against
heat / cold)
isorel *n(m)* hardboard
ivoire *n(m)* ivory (colour, material)

jack *n (m)* jack plug
jacuzzi ® *n(m)* Jacuzzi ®
jade *n(m)* jade (stone)
jambage *n(m)* door jamb; jamb; wedge
jardin *n(m)* garden
jardin *n(m)* **d'agrément** flower garden
jardinage *n(m)* gardening
jardinier (ière) *n(m)/(f)* gardener
jardinier (ière) *n(m)/(f)* **paysagiste** landscape
gardener

Jardinière à fleurs   Jute

jardinière *n(f)* **à fleurs** window box
jauge *n(f)* **de niveau d'huile** oil gauge
jaune *n(m)adj* yellow (colour)
jaune d'ocre *n(m)adj* yellow ochre (colour)
JCB ® *n(m)* JCB ® (excavator)
jerrican *n(m)* jerrycan
jet *n(m)* nozzle (pipe; tool)
jeter un coup d'œil sur *(or)* **à .....**
look-over (cast a glance at...)
jeu *n(m)* set (of tools, keys etc)
jeu *n(m)* **de clés** bunch of keys
joindre *v* to join (fix together)
joint *n(m)* joint (gen.); washer (for tap etc.)
joint *n(m)* **à recouvrement** lap joint
joint *n(m)* **à rotule** ball and socket joint
joint *n(m)* **bout à bout** butt joint
joint *n(m)* **de dilatation** expansion joint
jointoyer *v* to point (brickwork etc)
jointoyer *n(m)* pointing (brickwork etc)
joints *n(mpl)* (fam.) pointing
journée *adj* **(effectué dans la ~)** same-day
service
judas *n inv* door viewer (spyhole)
juste *adj* accurate (instrument)
jute *n(m)* jute

Kaolin   Kit

kaolin *n(m)* china clay
kit *n(m)* kit (for self assembly)
kit *adj (*en ~) flat-pack

lac *n(m)* lake
lâche *adj* loose (joint)
laine *n(f)* **de verre** glass wool
laine *n(f)* **minérale** rock wool
lait *n(m)* **de chaux** whitewash (for buildings)
laiton *n(m)* brass; tombac (alloy)
lambris *n(m)* cladding (panels)
lambris *n(m)* **de appui** wainscoting
lambrissé *adj* panelled (wall, door, ceiling)
lambrisser *v* to wainscot
lame *n(f)* blade (knife; tool); strip (of wood)
lame *n(f)* **d'arasement** wallpaper trimming tool
lame *n(f)* **de rasoir** razor blade
lame *n(f)* **de scie** saw blade
lame de ... blade of...
lame *n(f)* **persienne** louvre (single element)
lamelles *adj* **(à ~)** slatted (blinds etc)
lames *adj* **(en ~)** slatted (doors, furniture)
lamifié *n(m)* MDF (medium density fibreboard)
laminé *n(m)/adj* laminate (metal)
lampadaire *n(m)* standard lamp
lampe *n(f)* lamp; blowlamp
lampe *n(f)* **à arc** arc lamp; carbon arc lamp
lampe *n(f)* **à gaz** gas lamp; gaslight
lampe *n(f)* **à pétrole** oil lamp
lampe *n(f)* **de poche** torch; flashlamp
lampe *n(f)* **détecteur infrarouge** infrared security light
lampe *n(f)* **halogène** halogen lamp
lampe *n(f)* **témoin** pilot light
lampe-tempête *n(f)* storm lantern
lance-flammes *n(m)(inv)* flamethrower
lanterne *n(f)* lantern
laque *n(f)* lacquer; japan lacquer
laqué *adj* lacquered
laquer *v* to lacquer; to japan
laques *n(mpl)* lacquer ware
large *adj* wide; broad
largeur *n(f)* width; breadth

lasure *n(f)* stain (product)

latte *n(f)* floorboard; lath; woodblock (flooring material); batten (for floor, door)

latté *n(m)* block board

lavable *adj* washable

lavabo *n(m)* hand basin; washbasin; sink (bathroom); basin (for personal washing)

lavabo-colonne *n(f)* pedestal washbasin

lave-linge - sèche-linge *n(m)* washer-dryer

laveur (euse) *n(m)/(f)* **de carreaux** window cleaner (occupation)

lave-vaisselle *n(m)* dishwasher

légal *adj* legal

légal (est-il légal de faire?) legal (is it ~ to do?)

léger (ère) *adj(m)/(f)* light (little weight)

levier *n(m)* lever

liaison *n(f)* bond

libre-service *n(m)* **de vent en gros** cash and carry

liège *n(m)* cork (material)

liège *n(m)* **sur papier peint** cork textured wallpaper

ligne *n(f)* line (to define position); line (phone, elec.)

ligne *n(f)* **à haute tension** power line

ligne *n(f)* **de téléphone** telephone line

ligne *n(f)* **de terre** land-line (phone)

lilas *n(m)adj* lilac (shrub, colour)

lime *n(f)* file (tool)

lime *n(f)* **à double taille** crosscut file

lime *n(f)* **de précision** mini file

lime *n(f)* **mi-ronde** half round file

lime *n(f)* **plate (à main)** flat (hand) file

lime *n(f)* **tiers-point** triangular file

limer *v* to file (metal, timber)

limite *n(f)* **du terrain** boundary

lin *n(m)* linen

lino *n(m)* lino

linoléum *n(m)* linoleum

linteau *n(m)* lintel

liquide *n(m)*   liquid
liste *n(f)* **des prix**   price list
lit *n(m)*   bed
lit *n(m)* **de bébé**   cot
lit *n(m)* **du bas**   bunk bed (lower)
lit *n(m)* **du haut**   bunk bed (top)
lits *n(mpl)* **superposés**   bunk beds
livret *n(m)* **de l'utilisateur**   instruction book
locataire *n(m)/(f)* **à bail**   lease-holder
location *n(f)*   hire (machinery, vehicles); letting (of property); rental
logement *n(m)*   **dwelling; accommodation**
loggia *n(f)*   loggia
long (longue) *adj(m)/(f)*   long (gen.)
longtemps *adv*   long (a long time)
longueur *n(f)*   length
longueur *adj/adv* **(dans le sens de la ~)** lengthways
loquet *n(m)*   latch
loquet *n(m)* **à poucier**   door latch
loquet *n(m)* **automatique**   auto latch
loquet *n(m)* **étrier**   stirrup latch
loquet *v* **(soulever le ~ de ....)** to unlatch the …
lot *n(m)*   lot (in auction)
lotissement *n(m)*   small housing development
louer *v*   to let / to rent (property)
louer (à ~) *n*   (sign) to let / for hire
loupe *n(f)*   lens; magnifying glass
lourd *adj*   heavy
loyer *n(m)*   rent (for property)
lubrification *n(f)*   lubrication (general)
lucarne *n(f)*   attic window; dormer window; roof window; skylight; small window
lumière *n(f)*   light
lunette *n(f)* **de WC**   toilet seat
lunettes *n(fpl)* **de protection**   welding goggles
lunettes *n(fpl)* **de soudage**   welding goggles
lustre *n(m)*   chandelier

macadam *n(m)* tarmac / Tarmac ®
machette *n(f)* machete
machine *n(f)* machine (gen.)
machine *n(f)* **à laver** washing machine
machine à faire … machine for doing …
mâchoires *n(fpl)* jaws (of tool)
maçon *n(m)* builder (contractor); mason
maçonnerie *n(f)* masonry
magasin *n(m)* store (large shop)
magasin *n(m)* **de meubles** furniture store
magenta *n(m)adj* magenta (colour)
magnétoscope *n(m)* video-recorder
maillet *n(m)* mallet
main (à la ~) *adj* hand (by ~)
maire *n(m)* Mayor

Maison

maison *n(f)* house; home

~ à charpente en bois timber- framed
house
~ à colombage half-timbered house; timber-
framed house
~ bourgeoise mansion
~ de campagne cottage / house in the
  country
~ de maître manor house
~ de standing luxury home
~ de ville town house
~ familiale family home
~ individuelle detached house
~ jumelée semi-detached (house)
~ normande half-timbered house
~-témoin *n(f)* show-house
  maisonnette *n(f)* small house
  petite ~ : cottage

---

maître (esse) *n(m)/(f)* **d'œuvre** foreman,
forewoman

Maître *n(m)* (term of address for Notaire ≈ Sir / Master

mal (se faire ~) *v* to hurt (oneself)

mal fixé *adj* loose (not firmly fixed)

malaxer *v* to mix (cement; mortar etc)

manche *n(m)* handle; shaft (of tool)

manche long *adj* **(à ~)** long-handle (with a ~)

manchon *n(m)* straight connector (pipework)

mandrin *n(m)* chuck (of power drill)

manette *n(f)* lever (small)

manipuler *v* to handle (manipulate)

manœuvre *n(m)* labourer / workman (unskilled)

manoir *n(m)* country house; manor

manomètre *n(m)* pressure gauge

mansarde *n(f)* attic room

manteau *n(m)* **de cheminée** chimney breast; mantelpiece; mantelshelf

maquette *n(f)* **à l'échelle** scale model

marais *n(m)* marshland (wide area)

marbre *n(m)* marble (stone, objects)

marbrure *n(f)* marbling

marchand *n(m)* **de ferraille** scrap merchant

marchand (e) *n(m)/(f)* **en gros** wholesaler

marche *n(f)* stair; step

marché *n(m)* market

marécage *n(m)* marsh

marécageux (euse) *adj(m)/(f)* marshy

maréchal-ferrant *n(m)* blacksmith

marque *n(f)* make (trademark)

marron *n(m)adj* brown (colour)

marronnier *n(m)* **(d'Inde)** horse chestnut (tree)

Marteau

marteau *n(m)*   hammer

~ **à panne fendue**   claw hammer; carpenter's hammer

~ **arrache-clou**   claw hammer; carpenter's hammer

~ **de maçon**   club / lump hammer

~ **de porte**   door knocker

~ **de tapissier**   tack hammer

~ **perforateur**   hammer drill

masse *n(f)*   sledgehammer

massette *n(f)*   club / lump hammer

---

marteau *n(m)* **de porte**   door knocker
marteler *v*   to hammer (to beat)
masque *n(m)* **de protection**   welding mask
masquer *v*   to mask; to screen
masse *n(f)*   sledgehammer
massette *n(f)*   club / lump hammer
mastic *n(m)*   cement (for tiles); mastic; putty
masticage *n(m)*   grouting
mastiquer *v*   to putty
mat *adj*   matt (finish)
mât *n(m)*   flagpole; mast
matériaux *n(mpl)* **de construction**   building materials
mauvais *n(m)*   bad
mauvais état *adj*   poor condition
mauvaise odeur *n(f)*   bad smell
mauve *n(m)adj*   mauve (colour)
maximum *n(m)*   maximum
mazout *n(m)*   heating oil
mécanicien (ienne) *n(m)/(f)*   mechanic
mécanisme *n(m)*   mechanism
mèche *n(f)*   drill bit (for wood)
mèche *n(f)* **à bois**   wood drill; centre bit
meilleur (re) *n(m)/(f)*   best
mélamine *n(f)*   melamine

mélanger *v*   to mix (combine)
mélèze *n(m)*   larch (wood, tree)
membrane *n(f)*   membrane
meneau *n(m)*   mullion
menuiserie *n(f)*   carpentry; joinery
menuisier (ière) *n(m)/(f)*   joiner; carpenter
mercure *n(m)*   mercury
mesure *n(f)* **pliante**   folding ruler
mesurer *v*   to measure
métal *n(m)*   metal
métal *n(m)* **blanc**   white metal
métier *n(m)*   occupation; job; talent
mètre *n(m)*   meter (length) (Imperial =39.37in ; =3.28ft ; =1.09yd..)
mètre *n(m)* **ruban**   tape measure
métrique *adj*   metric
mettre *v*   to put
mettre *v* (item) **en place**   to fit (item) in place
mettre à terre *v*   to earth (elec.)
mettre du double vitrage à .... *v*   to double-glaze
meuble *n(m)*   item of furniture
meuble *adj*   soft land / ground
meuble *n(m)* **sous-vasque**   vanity unit
meuble *n(m)* **vitrine**   display cabinet
meubles *n(mpl)*   furniture
meubles *n(fpl)* **de chambre à coucher**   bedroom furniture
meule *n(f)*   grinding disk; grindstone
meuleuse *n(f)*   angle grinder
mica *n(m)*   mica
mieux *n inv*   better
mince *adj*   thin (not thick / fat)
mine *n(f)*   mine (ore / stone extraction)
minéral *n(m)*   mineral
minimum *n(m)*   minimum
minuterie *n(f)*   time switch
miroir *n(m)*   looking-glass; mirror
mitoyen (enne) *adj(m)/(f)*   dividing (wall etc.)
mitron *n(m)* **de cheminée**   chimney pot
mobile home *n(m)*   mobile home

mobilier *n(m)* furniture
mobilier *n(m)* **en rotin** cane furniture
mode *n(mpl)* **d'emploi** operating instructions
modèle *n(m)* pattern (template)
moderne *adj* modern
moderniser *v* to modernise
modification *n(f)* adjustment; alterations
modifications (apporter des ~ à ....) make
adjustment / alterations to ....
modifier *v* to alter (gen.)
moellon *n(m)* **creux** cavity block
moisissure *n(f)* mould
moitié *n(f)* half (one of two equal parts)
molette *n(f)* **coupante** pipe-cutter (hand tool)
monoxyde *n(m)* **de carbone** carbon
monoxide
monteur (euse) *n(m)/(f)* fitter (white goods)
monteur *n(m)* **d'échafaudages** scaffolder
monument *n(m)* **historique** historic / listed
building
moquette *n(f)* fitted carpet; **(~ avec un
envers en mousse)** foam backed carpet
mortaise *n(f)* mortise
mortier *n(m)* mortar
mortier *n(m)* **prêt à l'emploi** dry-mixed
mortar
mosaïque *n(f)* mosaic
moteur *n(m)* engine (internal combustion)
moteur *n(m)* **Diesel** diesel engine
motorisation *n(f)* **de porte / portail** remote
gate control
mouche *n(f)* fly (insect)
mouchetis *n(m)* pebbledash; rough
rendering; roughcast
moufle *n(f)* block and tackle
mouillant *n(m)* wetting agent
mouillé *adj* wet (damp - wall, floor)
moulage *n(m)* **sous pression** die-casting
moulé sous pression *adj* die-cast
moulin *n(m)* mill
moulin *n(m)* **à eau** water mill

Moulin à vent   Mycose fongique

moulin *n(m)* **à vent**   windmill
moulure *n(f)*   moulding (decorative feature)
mousse *n(f)*   moss
moussu *adj*   moss covered

Mur

mur *n(m)*   wall
~ **coupe-feu**   firewall
~ **creux**   cavity wall
~ **mitoyen**   dividing wall; party wall
~ **portant**   load-bearing wall

---

murer *v*   to wall; to brick up (fireplace, door)
mycose *n(f)* **fongique**   fungal infection

Négatif   Nord

négatif *n(m)*   negative (elec. polarity)
négociant n(m) **en bois**   timber merchant
néon *n(m)*   neon (light)
nettoyeur *n(m)* **haute pression**   high
pressure cleaner
neuf / neuve *adj(m)/(f)*   new (brand new)
neutre *adj*   neutral (elec. polarity)
niche *n(f)*   nook (for ornaments etc)
niveau *n(m)* **du sol**   ground level (access etc)
niveau *n(m)*   level (general); level (tool)
niveau *n(m)* **à bulle**   spirit level
nœud *n(m)*   knot (in wood, string)
noir *(m)*   black (colour)
noir *n(m)* **d'ébène**   ebony (colour)
nombre *n(m)*   number (figure(s))
non négligeable *adj*   sizeable (large object)
non-vente *n(f)*   no sale
nord *n(m)*   north; **(du côté** *(m)* ~ **)** north
side (land; wall)
nord *adj* **(exposé au** ~ **)**   north facing

Normale   Numéro de commande

normale *n(f)*   normal
norme *n(f)*   norm
normes britanniques *adj* **(conforme aux ~)** Imperial measure
notaire *n(m)* notary (≈ solicitor); (term of address for Notaire) **Maître** *n(m)* ≈ Sir / Master
note *n(f)* note (written record)
noté *pp/adj* noted (s'thing registered / recorded - an appointment, order for goods etc.)
noter *v* to note
nourrice *n(f)* jerrycan
nouveau (elle) *adj(m)/(f)* new (experience)
noyer *v*   to countersink (embed screw / bolt in surface)
noyer *v* to drench (in paste, paint etc)
noyer *n(m)* walnut (wood, tree)
nu *adj* bare (blade, wood, wire)
numérique *adj* digital
numéro *n(m)* number (house; tel; c. card)
numéro *n(m)* **de fax / télécopie** fax number
numéro (faire un ~) *v*   to dial (telephone a number)
numéro *n(m)* **de commande** order number

Oblong   Ordures

oblong (ongue) *adj (m)/(f)* oblong
ocre *n(m)adj* ochre (colour)
ocre brun *n(m)adj* terracotta (colour)
odeur *n(f)* odour; smell
œil-de-tigre *n(m)* tiger's eye (mineral)
œillet *n(m)* eyelet
ombragé *adj* shaded (by trees, awning)
ombre *n(f)* shade (shadow)
ondulé *adj* corrugated
onduleur *n(m)* inverter (elec.)
orage *n(m)* magnetic storm
orange *n(m)adj(inv)* orange (colour)
ordures *n(fpl)* rubbish (waste)

ordures *n(fpl)* **de jardinage** garden refuse
oriel *n(m)* bay window
orme *n(m)* elm (wood, tree)
orner *v* to ornament (building, structure)
ossature *n(f)* **métallique** metal frame (for partition)
où est.... où sont.... where is.... where are....
ouate *n(f)* cotton wool
ouest *n(m)* west; **(du côté** *(m)* **~)** west side
ouest *adj* **(exposé à l'~)** west facing
outil *n(m)* implement; tool
outil *n(m)* **électrique** power tool
ouvert *adj* open (opp. to 'closed')
ouverture *n(f)* opening
ouvrage *n(m)* building work
ouvrier *n(m)* **chargé de l'entretien** maintenance man
ouvrier (ière) *n(m)/(f)* worker (often linked to trade e.g.: **~ maçon** - building worker ; **~ menuisier** - carpenter)
ouvrier (ière) *n(m)/(f)* **dans le bâtiment** builder (employee)
ouvrir *v* to open; to unlock (using key)
ovale *adj* oval (shape)

pacage *n(m)* grazing
paddock *n(m)* paddock
pages *n(fpl)* **jaunes** ® Yellow Pages ®
paie *n(f)* pay (to general worker)
paiement *n(m)* payment
paille *n(f)* **de fer** steel wool; wire wool
paille *n(f)* **sur papier peint** straw textured wallpaper
palan *n(m)* hoist
pale *n(f)* blade (fan, propeller)
pâle *adj* pale (colour)

palier *n(m)* landing (staircase)
pancarte *n(f)* notice (sign)
panier *n(m)* basket (with handle)
panne *n(f)* purlin (construction); (machinery, vehicle) broken down
panneau *n(m)* panel
panneau *n(m)* **d'affichage** signboard
panneau *n(m)* **en aggloméré** fibreboard
panneau *n(m)* **solaire** solar panel
panneaux *adj* **(en ~)** panelled (room, fencing etc.)

Papier

papier *n(m)* paper

~ **à dessin** cartridge paper
~ **abrasif** abrasive paper
~ **adhésif** adhesive tape
~ **aluminium** aluminium foil
~ **d'apprêt** lining paper (wallpaper)
~ **de verre** glass paper; sandpaper

Papier peint

papier *n(m)* **peint** wallpaper

~ **lavable** wallpaper (washable)
~ **velouté** velvet textured wallpaper
~ **vinyle** vinyl wallpaper
~ **floqué** flock wallpaper
liège *n(m)* **sur ~** cork textured wallpaper

---

paquet *n(m)* package; packet; parcel
paraffine *n(f)* paraffin wax
parapet *n(m)* parapet
parasite *n(m)* parasite
paratonnerre *n(m)* lightning conductor
parc *n(mpl)* grounds (of private property)
parfum *n(m)* scent (flowers, perfume)
parfumer *v* to scent (flowers, perfume)
parpaing *n(m)* breeze block

parpaing *n(m)* **cellulaire** lightweight breeze block

parpaing *n(m)* **creux** hollow breeze block

parquet *n(m)* floor (wood block); parquet

parterre *n(m)* **de fleurs** flower bed

participer *v* **(faire ~)** to involve (cause participation)

pas *n(m)* **de porte** doorstep

passage *n(m)* passage (exterior)

passe *n(m)* passkey

passe-partout *n(m)/(inv)* master key; skeleton key

passe-plat *n(m)* service hatch

passer *v* to look in (pass by)

pâte *n(f)* paste (mixture)

pâte *n(f)* **à polir** polish (metal)

patio *n(m)* patio

pâturage *n(m)* pasture; grazing land

paumelle *n(f)* hinge (lift off / split)

paumelle *n(f)* **à rampe** hinge (lifting)

pavé *adj* paved

paver *v* to pave

pavés *n(mpl)* cobblestones

pavillon *n(m)* bungalow (gen.); villa (large town house)

payer *v* to pay; to settle (pay)

payer en espèces *v* pay in cash

payer (faire ~) *v* to charge (require payment)

paysage *n(m)* landscape

paysager (ère) *adj* open-plan (office)

paysagisme *n(m)* landscape gardening

peau *n(f)* **de chamois** chamois leather

peindre *v* to paint

peindre à l'aérosol *v* to spray-paint

peint à la main *adj* hand painted

peintre *n(m)* painter

peintre-décorateur *n(m)* painter-decorator

Peinture

peinture *n(f)* paint
~ **brillante** gloss paint
~ **coquille d'œuf** eggshell finish paint
~ **émulsion** emulsion paint
~ **en aérosol** aerosol paint; spray paint
~ **façade** masonry paint
~ **laquée** enamel paint
~ **mate** matt paint
~ **murale** wall painting
~ **satinée** satin paint

---

peinture-décoration *npl* painter(s) and
decorator(s) (business)
peintures *n(fpl)* paintwork
pelle *n(f)* shovel; spade (garden tool)
pelle *n(f)* **à poussière** dustpan
pelleteuse *n(f)* digger (mechanical);
shovel (mechanical)
pelote *n(f)* ball of string / yarn
pelouse *n(f)* lawn; cut grass
penderie *n(f)* walk in cupboard / wardrobe
pêne *n(m)* **demi-tour** sash (window) bolt
pente *n(f)* gradient; slope
penture *n(f)* strap hinge
percer *v* to drill (wood & substitutes)
perceuse *n(f)* **à main** hand drill
perceuse *n(f)* **à percussion** hammer drill
perceuse *n(f)* **électrique** power drill
perceuse-visseuse *n(f)* drill-screwdriver
perche *n(f)* pole
perçoir *n(m)* punch (timber, metal)
perdre *v* to lose (mislay)
perdu *adj* lost
permis *n(m)* **de construire** planning
permission; building permit
permis *n(m)* **de visiter** order to view
persienne *n(f)* louvred shutter
persienné *adj* louvred

pèse-personne *n(mpl)* bathroom scales
peser *v* to weigh
pétrole *n(m)* paraffin; kerosene
peuplier *n(m)* poplar (wood, tree)
phéniqué *adj* carbolic
pic *n(m)* pick (tool)
pichpin *n(m)* pitch-pine (wood, tree)
pièce *n(f)* room (gen.)
pied *n(m)* leg (furniture)
piédestal *n(m)* pedestal (statue)
pierre *n(f)* stone (mineral)
pierre *n(f)* **brute** gemstone
pierre *n(f)* **à aiguiser** grindstone; sharpening
stone; oilstone; whetstone (etc.)
pierre *n(f)* **abrasif** abrasive stone
pierre *n(f)* **angulaire** corner stone (for
building)
pierre *n(f)* **de bordure d'un trottoir**
kerbstone
pierre *n(f)* **de chaperon** coping stone
pieu *n(m)* stake (post, support)
pile *n(f)* battery (small appliances)
pile *n(f)* **solaire** solar cell
pilier *n(m)* pillar
pin *n(m)* pine (wood, tree)
pin *n(m)* **décapé** stripped pine (timber)
pince *n(f)* clip; pincers
pince *n(f)* **à décoffrer** wrecking bar (tool)
pince *n(fpl)* **à dénuder** wire / cable
strippers (elec.)
pince *n(f)* **à levier** wrecking bar (tool)
pince *n(f)* **à usages multiples** wire / cable
cutter / stripper
pince *n(f)* **crocodile** crocodile clip
pinceau *n(m)* paintbrush
pince-monseigneur *n(f)* crowbar; jemmy
(lever)
pinces *n(fpl)* pliers
pinces *n(fpl)* **à becs de longueur** long-nosed
pliers
pioche *n(f)* pick (tool)

Pioche

Plaquer

pioche *n(f)* **de cantonnier** mattock
pioche *n(f)* **hache** pickaxe
piquet *n(m)* peg (for awning, tent); stake
piquet *n(f)* **de clôture** post (fence)
piquet *n(m)* **de terre** earthing spike (elec.)
piscine *n(f)* swimming pool
piton *n(m)* screw eye
pistolet *n(m)* **à peinture** paint spray-gun
placage *n(m)* plating (metal coating); veneer
(surface layer)
placard *n(m)* cupboard; **(petit ~)** small
cupboard
placard *n(m)* **à vaisselle** china cabinet /
cupboard
place *n(f)* space (in building, car, etc)
placoplâtre ® *n(m)* plasterboard
plafond *n(m)* ceiling
plafonnier *n(m)* ceiling light; overhead light
plain *n(m)* lime pit
plan *n(m)* floor plan; level (surface); scheme
plan *n(m)* **de ...** design for ...
plan *n(m)* **de travail** work surface; work top
planche *n(f)* plank; floorboard
planche *n(f)* **à repasser** ironing board
planche *n(f)* **d'échafaudage** scaffold board
plancher *n(mpl)* floor; floor boards
planches *n(fpl)* boards; stage
plaque *n(f)* metal plate / sheet; name-plate
(of house)
plaque *n(f)* **d'applique** wall mounted bulb-
holder
plaque *n(f)* **d'amiante** asbestos mat
plaque *n(f)* **de plâtre** plasterboard
plaque *n(f)* **de plâtre ignifugée** fireproofed
plasterboard
plaque *n(f)* **de propreté** finger plate
plaque *n(f)* **de regard** manhole cover
plaque *n(f)* **renfort** reinforcing plate
plaqué *adj* metal plated (with precious metals)
plaquer *v* to plate (metal coating)

plaques *n(fpl)* **et poignées** *(fpl)* door furniture

plaquette *n(f)* **de parement** wall cladding

plastifié *adj* laminated (card)

plastique *n(m)* plastic

plat *adj* flat (horizontal); level (garden, ground)

plateau *n(m)* **de balance** pan / plate (of scales)

platine *n(f)* **pivotante** gate latch

platoir *n(m)* **à enduire inoxydable** stainless steel float (tool for plastering etc.)

plâtre *n(m)* plaster

plâtre *n(m)* **de Paris** plaster of Paris

plâtres *n(mpl)* plasterwork

plâtres *v* **(faire les ~)** to plaster

plâtrier *n(m)* plasterer

plein *adj* full

plein air *adj* **(de ~)** outdoor

plein air *adj* **(en ~)** open-air

plexiglas ® *n(m)* Perspex ®

plier *v* to bend (wire)

plinthe *n(f)* base board; skirting board; plinth

plomb *n(m)* fuse (elec.)

plomb *n(m)* lead (metal)

plomb *n(m)* **(à ~)** plumb (vertical)

plomb *adj* **(sans ~)** lead-free

plomberie *n(f)* plumbing

plombier *n(m)* plumber

plumeau *n(m)* feather duster

poêle *n(m)* stove (heater)

poêle *n(m)* **à bois** wood-burning stove

poids *n(m)inv* weight

poids *n(m)* **lourd** lorry (heavy ~)

poignée *n(f)* handle (of door, furniture)

poil *n(m)* bristle (single)

poil *n(m)* **de chameau** camel hair

poils *n(mpl)* bristles (on brush: synth.)

poinçonner *v* to use a punch (make a hole with hand tool)

point *n(m)* tack weld

point *n(m)* **d'ancrage** anchor position

point *n(m)* **de fusion** melting point
point *n(m)* **de référence** yardstick
point *n(m)* **mort** dead centre
pointage *n(m)* tack welding
pointe *n(f)* nail
pointe *n(f)* **annelée** annulated (ringed) nail
pointe *n(f)* **galvanisée** galvanised nail
pointer *v* to tack weld
polir *v* to polish (marble; stone)
polyéthylène *n(m)* polythene
polystyrène *n(m)* polystyrene
polystyrène *n(m)* **expansé** expanded
polystyrene
polyuréthane *n(m)* polyurethane
pomme *n(f)* **de douche** shower rose
pompe *n(f)* pump
pompe *n(f)* **à chaleur** heat pump
pompe *n(f)* **à graisse** grease gun
pompe *n(f)* **de circulation** circulating pump
pompe *n(f)* **de relevage** macerator
pompe *n(f)* **hydraulique à main pour**
déboucher drain plunger pump (hand pump to
unblock drains)
pomper *v* to pump
pompiers (sapeurs-~) *n(mpl)* fire service
ponçage *n(m)* sanding (making smooth)
poncer *v* to sand (make smooth)
ponceuse *n(f)* sanding machine
ponceuse *n(f)* **à bande** belt sanding
machine
ponceuse *n(f)* **excentrique** random orbit
sanding machine
ponceuse *n(f)* **vibrantes** orbital sanding
machine
pont-bascule *n(m)* weighbridge
porcelaine *n(f)* china (fine crockery)
porche *n(m)* porch
porcherie *n(f)* pigsty
portail *n(m)* gate (gen. decorative, elaborate)

Porte

porte *n(f)*   door; gate (of garden)
~ **coulissante** sliding door
~ **coupe-feu** fire door
~ **de derrière** back door
~ **d'écurie** stable door
~ **munie d'une moustiquaire** screen door
~ **persiennée** louvred door
~ **pliante** folding door
~-**fenêtre** *n(f)*   French door; patio doors

porte-clés *n(m)*   key-ring
porte-outils *n(m)*   tool rack
porter *v*   to carry
porteur (euse) *adj(m)/(f)*   load bearing
portique *n(m)*   portico
pose *n(f)* **de la toiture**   roofing (putting in place)
poser *v*   to fix (position); to put in place
poseur *n(m)* **de moquette**   carpet fitter
positif *n(m)*   positive (elec. polarity)
poste *n(f)* **à souder à la flamme**   gas welding kit
poste *n(f)* **à souder à l'arc**   arc welding kit
poste (mettre à la ~)   place in post box)
poster *v* to post (send by ~)
pot *n(m)*   pot (paint etc.)
pot *n(m)* **de peinture**   paint pot
poteau *n(m)*   pole; post; stake (substantial)
poteau *n(m)* **d'angle**   gatepost
poteau *n(m)* **télégraphique**   telegraph pole
poteau (x) *n(m)* **de clôture**   fence post
potence *n(m)* **porte-robinet**   tap bracket (wall mounting)
pou *n(m)*   louse (insect)
poubelle *n(f)*   dustbin; refuse bin
poubelle *n(f)* **à roulettes**   wheely-bin
pouce *n(m)*   inch (measure) = 2.54cm
poudre *n(f)* **à tracer**   chalk (powder)
pourpre *n(m)adj*   purple (colour – reddish)

pourri *adj*   rotten (decay)
pourrir *v*   to rot (decay)
pourrissant *adj*   rotting (decay)
pourriture *n(f)*   decay; rot
pourriture *n(f)* **humide**   wet rot
pourriture *n(f)* **sèche**   dry rot
pousser *v*   to wheel (barrow, cart)
poussière *n(f)*   dust
poutre *n(f)*   beam
poutre *n(f)* **en fer**   RSJ (rolled steel joist)
poutre *n(f)* **en treillis**   lattice girder
poutrelle *n(f)* **en 'H'**   H-beam
pré *n(m)*   pasture (grassland)
préavis *n(m)*   notice (warning, instruction)
premier étage *n(m)*   first floor
première classe (de ~) *adj*   first class
premiers soins *n(mpl)*   first aid
prendre *v* **(faire ~)**   to set; to cure (concrete, mixture)
prendre *v* **le courant** *n*   to have an electric shock
preneur (euse) *n(m)/(f)*   lessee (acquirer of lease)
presbytère *n(m)*   manse
préserver *v*   to preserve
pression *n(f)*   pressure
prêt à gâcher *adj*   dry-mix (for concrete, mortar etc.) ready-to-mix

---

Prise

In general a point of connection or supply to one of several utilities. The word 'prise' is qualified by details of its precise purpose.

prise *n(f)*

~ **de courant**   power point; socket
~ **à deux fiches**   two pin plug (elec.)
~ **à encastrer**   recessed socket
~ **à trios fiches**   three pin plug (elec.)

Prise (continued)

prise *n(f)*
- **~ d'eau** hydrant
- **~ d'air** air vent
- **~ de téléphone** telephone socket
- **~ de télévision** television socket
- **~ de terre** earthed socket
- **~ de vidange** washing machine waste outlet
- **~ double** double socket (elec.)
- **~ électrique** electric socket
- **~ en appliqué** socket (surface mounted)
- **~ pour rasoir électrique** shaver point / socket

Prix   **Protège du vent**

Prix

prix *n(m)* charge; cost; price;
- **~ au catalogue** list price
- **~ coûtant** cost price
- **~ de gros** wholesale price
- **~ de vente** selling price
- **à ~ modéré** *adj* at a mid-price
- **à bas ~** *adj* at a low-priced

problèmes *n(mpl)* **cardiaques** heart trouble
produit *n(m)* **anticorrosion** anticorrosive
produit *n(m)* **pour nettoyer des vitres**
window cleaner (chemical)
profond *adj* deep
profondeur *n(f)* depth
projecteur *n(m)* spotlight
projet *n(m)* scheme
prolonger *v* to lengthen (objects)
propane *n(m)* propane
propriétaire *n(m)/(f)* home owner; land
owner; landlord / landlady
protection *n(f)* pad (support, protect)
protège du vent *adj* wind protection / proof

Psyché   Purgeur d'air

psyché *n(f)*   cheval glass
puisard *n(m)*   soakaway
puissance *n(f)*   wattage (elec.)
puits *n(m)*   well (pit for water); shaft (vent)
pulvériser *v*   to spray (fluid, paint)
punaise *n(f)*   drawing pin
purgeur *n(m)* **d'air**   central heating air valve

Quart   Quincaillier

quart *n(m)*   quarter (one fourth)
quartz *n(m)*   quartz (mineral)
quatre temps *adj*   four-stroke (engine)
queue *n(f)*   handle (saucepan; frying pan)
Quiès ® *npl*   ear plugs
quincaillerie *n(f)*   hardware shop;
ironmongery
quincaillier (ère) *n(m)/(f)*   hardware dealer;
ironmonger

rabattable *adj* hinged (seat)
rabot *n(m)* wood plane
rabot *n(m)* **Surform** ® Surform ® (tool)
raboter *v* to shave (with plane)

Raccord

raccord *n(m)* connector; joint (pipe ~)

~ **à olive** compression joint / connector (for
   metal pipes with 'olive' seals)
~ **à souder** soldered joint / connector
~ **coude** elbow connector
~ **courbe** angle connector
~ **cuivre** copper pipe joint
~ **cuivre à souder** capillary (soldered)
copper
   pipe joint
~ **de gaz** gas connector (for appliances using
   bottle gas)
~ **d'évacuation souple** waste pipe (flexible)
~ **droit** straight connector
~ **droit (réduction)** straight reducing
   connector
~ **raccord** *n(m)* **instantané** compression
   joint / connector
~ **sortie lavabo** wash basin outlet connector
~ **té égal** 'T' joint (all equal diam.)
~ **té inégal** 'T' joint (various diam.)
~ **tuyau de vidange** waste pipe connector

---

racloir *n(m)* scraper (tool)(decorating etc); paint
stripper (tool)
radiateur *n(m)* radiator (heating)
radiateur *n(m)* **électrique à accumulation**
storage heater (elec.)
rail *n(m)* **à rideaux** curtain rail
rail *n(m)* **métallique** metal rail (for partition)
rainé *adj* grooved
rainure *n(f)* groove (carpentry, masonry);
rabbet

Rallonge Registre

rallonge *n(f)* extension cable
rallonge *n(f)* **téléphonique** telephone
extension cable
ramassage *n(m)* **des ordures** rubbish
collection
ramin *n(m)* ramin (timber)
ramoneur *n(m)* chimney sweep
rampe *n(f)* banister; handrail; ramp (in gen.,
for access)
rangement *n(m)* storage (unit, space)
râpe *n(f)* rasp (tool)
raser *v* to level (knock down)
rasoir *n(m)* razor
rat *n(m)* rat
rayon *n(m)* radius; department (in a store);
shelf (in shop)
rayonnage *n(m)* shelving
réaménager *v* to redecorate
rebord *n(m)* **de fenêtre** windowsill
reboucher *v* to fill (crack, hole)
reboucheur *n(m)* filler (product)
receveur *n(m)* **de douche** shower tray
recevoir une facture *v* to receive an invoice
réchaud *n(m)* **à gaz** gas ring (portable)
rêche *adj* rough (surface)
reconstruction *n(f)* reconstruction;
rebuilding
reconstruire *v* to reconstruct; to rebuild
recouvrir partiellement *v* to overlap
rectangle *n(m)* oblong
rectangulaire *adj* oblong
réévaluation *n(f)* revaluation
réévaluer *v* to revalue
refaire *v* **l'installation électrique** to rewire
refendre *v* to split
regard *n(m)* manhole
regarder *v* to look at
région *n(f)* **d'exploitation minière** mining
area
registre *n(m)* damper (in fireplace)

Réglable   Réservoir de fioul

réglable *adj*   adjustable (height etc)
réglage *n(m)*   adjustment
règle *n(f)*   rule (measure)
règle *n(f)* **plate graduée**   straightedge rule
règlement *n(m)*   payment (to settle account)
règlements *n(mpl)* **d'urbanisme**   planning regulations
régler *v*   to settle (pay)
réglet *n(f)* **inox flexible**   coiled spring rule
réglette *n(f)* **fluorescente**   fluorescent tube holder
relations *n(fpl)* **du travail**   labour relations
remblayer *v*   to fill (ditch, hollow)
rembourrage *n(m)*   padding
rembourré *adj*   padded (material)
remise *n(f)*   shed (garden)
remise *n(f)* **à bois**   woodshed
remorque *n(f)*   trailer (towed cart)
rémouleur (euse) *n(m)/(f)*   knife sharpener (occupation)
rencontre *n(f)*   meeting
renforcer *v*   to brace (wall; structure)
rénovation *n(f)*   renovation
rénover *v*   to renovate; to refurbish
réparable *adj*   repairable
réparateur (trice) *n(m)/(f)*   repair man / woman
réparation *n(f)*   repair
réparer *v*   to repair; to mend
repassage *n(m)*   ironing
repeindre *v*   to repaint
repeindre et retapisser *v*   to redecorate (paintwork & wallpaper)
répondeur *n(m)* **téléphonique**   answerphone
représentant (e) *n(m)/(f)*   sales rep. / representative
réseau *n(m)*   network; system (utilities, transport).
réseau *n(m)* **d'égout**   sewage system
réservoir *n(m)*   tank (general use)
réservoir *n(m)* **de fioul**   fuel tank

réservoir *n(m)* **du chasse d'eau** cistern (of WC)

résistant à la chaleur *adj* heat proof

respiration *n(f)* breathing

responsable *n(m)/(f)* person in charge (of shop, business etc.); manager

ressort *n(m)* **à cintrer** pipe bending spring

restitution *n(f)* restoration (of building)

retapisser *v* to repaper

retrouver *v* to locate (find)

réunir *v* to join (fix together)

réveille-matin *n(m)* alarm clock

revêtement *n(m)* cladding; coating (paint, plaster); covering (wall, floor); casing

revêtement *n(m)* **de piscine** pool liner

revêtement *n(m)* **de sol** floor covering

revêtement *n(m)* **en bois** timber cladding

revêtement *n(m)* **mural** wall covering

revêtement *n(m)* **protecteur** preservative (for timber)

revêtu de bois *adj* timber-clad

révisée (être ~) *v* to be serviced (appliance)

révision *n(f)* service (maintenance)

rez-de-chaussée *n(m)(inv)* ground-floor

risque *n(m)* **d'incendie** fire hazard

rivet *n(m)* rivet (metal fixing)

rivet *n(m)* **à tête ronde** round-head rivet

rivetage *n(m)* **par recouvrement** lap riveting

riveter *v* to rivet

Robinet

robinet *n(m)* tap (gas, water)

~ **à flotteur** float valve (WC)

~ **auto perceur** tap (self fixing)

~ **d'arrêt** stopcock; stop tap

~ **de gaz** gas tap

Robinet (continued)

robinet *n(m)* tap (gas, water)

~ **de purge** bleed valve

~ **de vidange** drain tap

~ **mélangeur** mixer tap

Ronce de noyer   Ruban adhésif ...

ronce *n(f)* **de noyer** burr walnut (timber)

rondelle *n(f)* washer (metal, for bolts etc)

rondelle *n(f)* **cuvette** cup washer

rondelle *n(f)* **Grower** split washer

rosace *n(f)* ceiling rose (decorative plaster);
rose window

rose *n(m)adj* rose (colour)

rose (bois *n(m)* **de** ~ **)** rosewood (timber)

rose *n(m)adj* **vif** shocking pink (colour)

rotin *n(m)* cane (material)

roue *n(f)* wheel (for vehicle etc.)

roue *n(f)* **à rochet** ratchet wheel

roue *n(f)* **hydraulique** water wheel

rouge *n(m)adj* red (colour)

rouge-brun *n(m)adj(inv)* puce (colour)

rouge *n(m)adj* **cerise** cherry (colour)

rouge *n(m)adj(inv)* **feu** flame-coloured

rouge *n(m)adj* **rubis** ruby (colour)

rouille *n(f)* rust

rouille *adj* **(anti-**~ **)** rust-proof

rouillé *adj* rusted; rusty

rouleau *n(m)* **de peintre** paint roller

roulette *n(f)* small wheel; castor (furniture
wheel)

roulette *n(f)* **colleur ébonite** wallpaper seam
roller

roulette *n(f)* **d'arasement** wallpaper trimming
wheel

route (petite ~ **)** *n(f)* lane (minor road)

routier *n(m)* lorry driver

ruban *n(m)* **adhésif de masquage** masking
tape

ruban *n(m)* **Téflon ® d'étanchéité** joint
sealing tape (PTFE)
ruelle *n(f)* lane (in town)
rugosité *n(f)* roughness
rugueux (euse) *adj(m)/(f)* rough
ruine *n(f)* ruin (building)
ruines *adj* **(en ~)** ruined; derelict
rustique *adj* rustic (timber products)

sablage *n(m)* sandblasting

Sable

sable *n(m)* sand (as beach)

~ **argenté** silver sand

~ **de rivière** river sand

~ **doux** soft sand

~ **en vrac** sand (loose, in bulk)

~ **fin** fine sand

~ **grossier** coarse sand

~ **liant** sharp sand

---

sableuse *n(f)* sandblaster (machine)

sableuse *v* **(décaper à la ~)** to sandblast clean

sablière *n(f)* sandpit (quarry)

sac *n(m)* sack (large bag)

sac *n(m)* **de sable** sandbag

sac *n(m)* **poubelle** bin liner

salaire *n(m)* pay (professional)

salarié (e) *n(m)/(f)* employee

saletés *n(fpl)* rubbish (junk)

salle *n(f)* **à manger** dining room

salle *n(f)* **de bains** bathroom

salle *n(f)* **des fêtes** village hall

salon *n(m)* living room; lounge (of house, flat)

salon (petit ~) *n(m)* parlour

salopette *n(f)* dungarees; overalls

sanitaire *adj* sanitary (fittings)

santal *n(m)* sandalwood (wood, tree)

sapin *n(m)* deal (timber); fir (tree)

sapinette *n(f)* spruce pine (wood, tree)

sarcler *v* to hoe (plants; flowerbed)

saule *n(m)* willow (wood, tree)

sauter (faire ~ les plombs) *v* to fuse (to blow the fuses)

savon *n(m)* soap (cleaning)

savon *n(m)* **phéniqué** carbolic soap

scellé *n(m)* seal (tight closure)

sceller *v* to seal
schéma *n(m)* diagram
schéma *n(m)* **de circuit** circuit diagram (elec.)

Scie

scie *n(f)* saw (tool)

~ **à chantourner** coping / fret saw
~ **à découper** fretsaw
~ **à denture américaine** fine tooth saw
~ **à dos** tenon saw
~ **à guichet** keyhole saw / pad saw
~ **à métaux** hacksaw
~ **à monture de menuisier** frame saw
~ **à onglet** mitre saw; tenon saw
~ **à panneaux** panel saw
~ **à placage** veneer saw
~ **à refendre** rip saw
~ **à ruban** band saw
~ **à ruban de précision** scroll saw
~ **circulaire** circular saw; buzz saw
~ **clocher** hole saw
~ **de charpentier** carpenters saw
~ **de travers** crosscut saw
~ **égoïne** hand saw
~ **égoïne universelle** multi-purpose saw
~ **électrique** power saw
~ **grosse coupe** large tooth saw
~ **manuelle** hand saw
~ **sauteuse** jig saw

---

scier *v* saw (to)
scierie *n(f)* timber yard
sciure *n(f)* sawdust
scories *n(fpl)* slag (from metal furnace)
scotch ® *n(m)* Sellotape ®
Scotch ® *n(m)* adhesive tape
sculpter *v* to sculpt
seau *n(m)* bucket; pail
sécateur *n(mpl)* secateurs

séchoir *n(m)* **parapluie** rotary clothes line
secours *n(m)* help; assistance
secours *n(m)* **d'urgence** emergency aid
secrétaire *n(m)* writing desk
secteur *n(m)* **en expansion** growth area
semelle *n(f)* fence post holder / sole
plate (metal)
semelle *n(f)* **boulonnée** fence post holder /
sole plate (metal, bolt fixed)
semelle *n(f)* **sur piquet métallique** fence
post holder / sole plate (with metal stake)
semence *n(f)* upholstery nail; tin-tack
semi. / semi- remorque *n(m)* lorry (artic /
articulated ~)
sentier *n(m)* pathway (narrow)
sentir *v* to smell
serre *n(f)* greenhouse; (also) claw
serre *n(f)* **chaude** hothouse
serre-câble *n(m)* cable clip
serre-jointe *n(f)* clamp
serrer *v* to clamp
serre-tubes *n(m)* pipe wrench
serrure *n(f)* lock (key operated)
serrure *n(f)* **de sûreté** latching lock; Yale ®
lock
serrure *n(f)* **pêne demi-tour** sashlock
serrure *n(f)* **encastrée** inset lock
serrurier *n(m)* locksmith
service *n(m)* **d'assistance** helpdesk;
helpline
Service *n(m)* **des Ponts et Chaussées**
Highways Department
shale *n(m)* shale (mineral)
siège *n(m)* seat (furniture)
sièges *n(mpl)* **de salon** lounge suite (furniture)
silencieux (ieuse) *adj(m)/(f)* noiseless
silicone *n(f)* silicone
siphon *n(m)* waste trap
siphon *n(m)* **avec tube droit** upstand (water
supply)

siphon *n(m)* **démontable** WC siphon (unit in separate components)

siphon *n(m)* **monobloc** siphon (WC - integrated unit)

siphonner *v* to siphon

sisal *n(m)* sisal

site *n(m)* **d'enfouissement des déchets** landfill site

smille *n(f)* mason's pick

société *n(f)* **de crédit immobilier** building society

socle *n(m)* base (of a fitting, appliance); pedestal (statue)

soies *n(fpl)* bristles (on brush etc.: real)

soin *n(m)* **(avec ~)** care (with ~)

sol *n(m)* floor; ground; soil

sol *adj* **(au ~)** earthed (elec.)

sol *n(m)* **(sous-~)** basement

solide *n(m)* solid

solide *adj* firm (solid)

solive *n(f)* joist

solive *n(f)* **de plafond** ceiling joist

solution *n(f)* solution (liquid mixture)

solution *n(f)* **acide pour piles** battery acid

solvant *n(m)* solvent (liquid)

sombre *adj* dark (room, paint); dim (poorly lit)

sommet *n(m)* apex

sommier *n(m)* bed base

sonnerie *n(f)* buzzer

sonnette *n(m)* door bell

sonnette *n(f)* **d'alarme** alarm bell

sortie *n(f)* **de secours** fire exit

souche *n(f)* tree stump

soudage *n(m)* welding

soudage *n(m)* **à arc** arc welding

soudage *n(m)* **par points** spot-weld

soude *n(f)* soda (chemical)

souder *v* to solder; to weld

souder (poste *n(f)* **à ~ à la flamme)** gas welding kit

soudeur *n(m)* **à arc** arc welder

soudure *n(f)*   solder (metal alloy)
soudure *n(f)* **à l'étain**   soft solder
soudure *n(f)* **à recouvrement**   lap welding
soulever *v*   to lift
soupape *n(f)*   valve
soupape *n(f)* **de sécurité**   safety valve
soupape *n(f)* **d'échappement**   outlet valve
sourcier (ière) *n(m)/(f)*   water diviner
sourcier (ière) *n(m)/(f)* **radiesthésiste**   water diviner
souricière *n(f)*   mousetrap
souris *n(f)*   mouse
spatule *n(f)*   spatula
spécialiste *n(m)/(f)*   expert
spécification *n(f)*   specification (for construction etc)
spécification *n(f)* **du modèle**   design specification
stationnement (aire *n(f)* **de ~)**   parking area / apron
stériles *n(mpl)*   slag (burnt solid fuel)
store *n(m)*   window blind
store *n(m)* **sur pied**   awning on legs
store enroulé *n(m)*   roller blind
store vénitien *n(m)*   Venetian blind
stratifié *n(f)*   laminate (plastic)
stratifié *adj*   laminated (plastic)
stuc *n(m)*   stucco (rendering, decorative plasterwork)
stylo *n(m)* **colle**   glue pen
sud *n(m)*   south; **(du côté** *n(m)* **~)**   south side
sud *adj* **(exposé au ~)**   south-facing
suie *n(f)*   soot
suintement *n(m)*   seepage (small flow)
suinter *v*   to seep (small flow)
superficie *n(f)*   area (of land); floor area
superflu *adj*   unwanted (material, product)
supplément *n(m)*   extra charge; **(sans ~)**   no extra charge
support *n(m)*   brace (hold up)

surcharge *n(f)* overload (elec., gen.)
surcharger *v* to overload
surestimation *n(f)* overestimate
surface *n(f)* **(en ~)** above ground
surplomb *adj* overhanging
sycomore *n(m)* sycamore (wood, tree)
sylvestre *adj* silvan
système *n(m)* **d'alimentation en eau** water system
système *n(m)* **d'assainissement** drainage system
système *n(m)* **de chauffage** heating system
système *n(m)* **d'extinction automatique** sprinkler system

table *n(f)* table
table *n(f)* **à tapissier** pasting table
table *n(f)* **de cuisson** hob (elec. stove)
table *n(f)* **de cuisson en vitrocéramique** ceramic hob
table *n(f)* **de salle à manger** dining table
table *n(m)* **de travail** work table
tableau *n(m)* **de commande** main switch-board
tableau *n(m)* **de fusibles** fuse board
tableau *n(m)* **de répartition** consumer unit
tableau *n(m)* **noir** blackboard; chalkboard
tablette *n(f)* shelf
tablier *n(m)* apron (clothing)
tablier *n(m)* **de soudeur** welding apron
tache *n(f)* mark; stain (gen. discoloration);
tâche *n(f)* job (task)
tâche *adj* **(à la ~)** jobbing
tacher *v* to mark; to stain
taillader *v* to hack (strike at)
taille-haies *n(m)inv* hedge trimmer (power)

tailler *v* to hack off; to make (to a pattern / design)

tailler d'onglet *v* to mitre

tailler en biseau *v* to bevel (an edge e.g. mirror)

tailler *v* to carve

taloche *n(f)* float (plasterers tool); hawk (trowel with handle underneath)

taloche *n(f)* **bois** float (wooden)

tampon *n(m)* rubber stamp

tampon *n(m)* **Jex ®** Brillo ® pad

tapis *n(m)* carpet

tapis *n(m)* **de bain** bath mat

tapissier (ière) *n(m)/(f)* upholsterer

taquet *n(m)* cleat

tarière *n(f)* **à gouge** bradawl

tarter *n(m)* lime scale

tartière *n(f)* gimlet

tas *n(m)* **de bois** woodpile

technicien *n(m)* **de maintenance** service engineer

teck *n(m)* teak (wood, tree)

teinture *n(f)* **d'iode** iodine (antiseptic)

télécommande *n(f)* remote control

télécopie *n(f)* fax

télécopier *v* to fax

télécopieur *n(m)* fax machine

tenon *n(m)* tenon (e.g. 'mortise and tenon'

tension *n(f)* voltage

tension (basse ~) *n(f)* low voltage

tension (haute ~) *n(f)* high voltage

tension (sous ~) *adj* live (elec. circuit)

tension *n(f)* **de secteur** mains voltage

térébenthine *n(f)* turpentine / turps

termite *n(m)* termite

ternir *v* to fade; to tarnish

ternissure *n(f)* tarnish

terrain *n(m)* ground (area)

terrain *n(m)* **à bâtir** building land / plot

terrain *n(m)* **marécage** marshland

terrain *n(m)* **vierge** green field site

terrasse *n(f)* terrace (exterior leisure area); patio; outside

terrasse *adv* **(à la ~)** outdoor (on patio or formal area)

terrasses (en ~) *adj* terraced (garden, landscape)

terre *n(f)* ground (land); soil; earth (elec.); **(sous ~)** below ground; underground (cable, wire)

terre *n(f)* **cuite** terracotta (material)

terre *n(f)adj* **de Sienne brûlée** burnt sienna (colour)

terre *n(f)adj* **d'ombre brûlée** burnt umber (colour)

tester *v* to trial (to try out)

testeur *n(m)* **de tension** circuit tester (elec.)

texture *n(f)* texture (of surface)

thermocouple *n(m)* thermocouple

thermomètre *n(m)* thermometer

thermopompe *n(f)* heat pump

thermostat *n(m)* thermostat

thibaude *n(f)* carpet underlay

tiède *adj* lukewarm

tige *n(f)* rod

tilleul *n(m)* lime (wood, tree)

tire-fond *n(m)* coach bolt / screw

tiroir *n(m)* drawer (furniture)

tissu *n(m)* fabric

tissu *n(m)* **sur papier peint** fabric textured wallpaper

toile *n(f)* canvas (material)

toile *n(f)* **cirée** oilcloth

toile *n(f)* **de jute** hessian

toile *n(f)* **émeri** emery cloth

toile *n(f)* **métallique** wire cloth; wire gauze

toilettes *n(fpl)* lavatory

toit *n(m)* roof

toit *n(m)* **de chaume** thatched roof

toit-terrasse *n(m)* flat roof

toiture *n(f)* roofing (material)

tôle *n(f)* metal sheet; metal plating (protection on doors etc.)

tôle *n(f)* **ondulée** corrugated iron
tombac *n(m)* tombac (alloy)
ton *n(m)* shade (of colour)
tondeuse *n(f)* lawnmower
tondeuse *n(f)* **à gazon** lawnmower
tondeuse *n(f)* **à moteur** motor mower
tondeuse *n(f)* **électrique** electric lawnmower
tonneau *n(m)* wine cask
tour *n(f)* tower (building, gen.)
tour *n(m)* **à banc** bench lathe
tour *n(m)* **à bois** lathe for wood-turning
tour *n(m)* **à métaux** lathe for metalwork
tour *n(m)* **revolver** turret lathe
tournage *n(m)* turning (with a lathe)
tourne-à-gauche *n(m)/(inv)* wrench (tool)
tournevis *n(m)* screwdriver
tournevis *n(m)* **cruciforme** cross-head
screwdriver
tournevis *n(m)* **d'électricien** electrician's
screwdriver
tournevis *n(m)* **pour vis Philips ®** Phillips ®
screwdriver
tournevis *n(m)* **testeur** screwdriver-tester
(elec.)
tout *pro* the lot (everything)
tractopelle *n(f)* excavator; JCB ®
traité thermiquement *adj* heat treated
traitement *n(m)* **antirouille** rustproofing
traitement *n(m)* **des déchets** waste disposal
traiter *v* to handle (deal with)
tranchant *adj* sharp (chisel, knife)
tranchée *n(f)* trench
tranchée *v* **(creuser une ~)** to dig a trench
transformateur *n(m)* transformer
transformer *v* to alter (building)
translucide *adj* translucent
transparent *adj* transparent
transport *n(m)* **routier** haulage
transporteur *n(m)* carrier; haulier
trappe *n(f)* trapdoor
trappe *n(f)* **d'access** access hatch

trappe *n(f)* **(du grenier)** hatch (loft ~)
travail *n(m)* job (available work)
travailleur (euse) *n(m)/(f)* workman/woman
(gen. worker / hard worker)
travailleur (euse) *n(m)/(f)* **à la tâche** jobber
travaux *n(mpl)* **de décoration** decorating
works) to improve appearance of building /
property etc.)
travaux *n(mpl)* **de peinture** redecoration
travers *adj* **(de ~)** skewed; crooked
treillis *n(m)* lattice
treillis *n(m)* **métallique** wire mesh
tremper *v* to soak; to wet
trépan *n(m)* trepan (cylindrical saw)
tréteau *n(m)* trestle
treuil *n(m)* winch
triangle *n(m)* triangle (shape)
trimballer *v* to cart
tringle *n(f)* curtain rail; metal rod
tringle *n(f)* **à rideaux** curtain pole
tringle *n (f)* **d'escalier** stair rod
tronc *n(m)* **d'arbre** tree trunk
tronçonneuse *n(f)* chainsaw
trop-plein *n(m)* overfull (sink, bath etc.)
trou *n(m)* hole (in timber, clothing)
trou *n(m)* **de serrure** keyhole
trou *n(m)* **de souris** mouse-hole
trousse *n(f)* **à outils** tool bag; tool kit
truc *n(m)* stuff (unspecified material)
truelle *n(f)* trowel
truelle *n(f)* **à joints** pointing trowel
truelle *n(f)* **de briqueteur** bricklayers trowel
trumeau *n(m)* overmantel
tube *n(m)* tube (pipe); (container for glue etc.)
tube *n(f)* **(coupe-~)** tube / pipe cutter
tube *n(m)* **cuivre** copper tube / pipe
tube *n(m)* **fluorescente** fluorescent tube
tube *n(m)* **plastique** plastic tube / pipe
tuile *n(f)* roof tile
tuile *n(f)* **faîtière** ridge tile
tuiles *v* **(poser des ~)** to tile (on roof)

turquoise *n/adj(f)* turquoise (colour)
tuteur *n(m)* **(mettre un ~ à…** stake / support
for a plant / tree etc. (in garden)

Tuyau

tuyau *n(m)* pipe; flue (of stove, boiler)

~ **cuivre** copper pipe
~ **d'arrosage** hosepipe
~ **de descente** down pipe
~ **de poêle** stovepipe
~ **de trop-plein** overflow pipe
~ **de vidange** waste pipe
~ **d'écoulement** soil pipe
~ **d'entrée** inlet pipe
 ~ **plastique** plastic pipe

UE *n(f)* EU European Union
union *n (f)* union (threaded pipe connector)
Union *n(f)* **européenne** European Union
unité *n(f)* **calorifique** BTU (British Thermal
Unit)
urbanisme *n(m)* town planning
usine *n(f)* factory
utile *adj* useful (of assistance)
utiliser *v* to use (a machine, tool)

va-et-vient *n(m)* **(interrupteur de ~)** two-way switch

vaisselier *n(m)* dresser (displaying china)

vaisselle *n(f)* crockery

vanne *n(f)* ball valve; gate valve

vanne *n(f)* **d'arrêt** stop valve

vantail (aux) *n(m)* shutter (single leaf of ~)

vapeur *n(f)* steam (water vapour)

vaporisateur *n(m)* vaporiser

vaporiser *v* to spray (fluid, paint); to vaporise

variateur *n(m)* **d'ambiance** dimmer-switch

variateur *n(m)* **de lumière** dimmer switch

vasistas *n(m)* louvres (in window)

vasque *n(f)* built-in washbasin; vanity basin

va-vite *adj* **(construit à la ~)** jerry-built; **(fait à la ~)** slapdash (workmanship)

veiné *adj* veined (showing grain)

Velcro ® *n(m)* Velcro ®

vendeur (euse) *n(m)/(f)* salesperson; seller

vendre *v* to sell

vendre tout *v* to sell up

vent *n(m)* wind (weather)

vente *n(f)* selling

vente *n(f)* **en gros** wholesale

ventilateur *n(m)* fan (for cooling)

ventilateur *n(m)* **d'extraction** extractor fan

ventilation *n(f)* ventilation (building, room)

ventilé *adj* **(non-~)** unventilated (room etc)

ventouse *n(f)* drain plunger (rubber hemisphere)

ver *n(m)* **à bois** woodworm

véranda *n(f)* conservatory

verger *n(m)* orchard

vérifié *v* checked

vérifier *v* to check (verify)

vermeil (eille) *adj* *(m)/(f)* rose-red (colour)

vermiculite *n(f)* vermiculite

vermiculite *n(f)* **(granulé isolant ~)** granulated vermiculite

vermoulu *adj* woodworm ridden

vermoulure *n(f)* wormhole (furniture, timber)

Verni   Vinyle

verni *adj* varnished
vernir *v* to varnish; to japan
vernis *n(m)* varnish
vernissage *n(m)* varnishing

Verre

verre *n(m)* glass (gen.)

~ **vitre** plate glass
~ **à vitres** window panes
~ **armé** wired glass
~ **coloré** stained glass (product)
~ **de sécurité** safety / shatterproof glass

---

verrière *n(f)* glass roof

Verrou

verrou *n(m)* bolt (to secure door / window)

verrou *n(m)* lock (secured with bolt)

~ **à bouton** deadbolt (activated with button)
~ **à clé** key operated (mortise) deadlock
~ **haut sécurité** high security lock
~ **de sûreté** double (safety) lock

---

verrouiller *v* to bolt; to lock (with bolt)
vert *n(m)adj* **émeraude** emerald green (colour)
vert *n(m)adj* **jade** jade (colour)
vert *n(m)adj(inv)* **mousse** moss green (colour)
vestibule *n(m)* entrance (lobby)
vide *adj* empty
vidéo *n(f)* video
vide-ordures *n(fpl)* refuse chute; rubbish chute
vider *v* to empty
vilebrequin *n(m)* brace and bit
villa *n(f)* villa (holiday home)
village *n(m)* village (small community)
vinyle *n(m)* vinyl (material)
violet *n(m)adj* (colour) violet; (bluish) purple

Vis

vis *n(f)*   screw (means of fixing)

~ **à bois**   wood screw

~ **à cheville expansible**   expansion bolt

~ **à tête etoile**   easydrive screw

~ **à tête fendue**   slotted screw

~ **à tête fraisée**   countersunk screw

~ **à tête fraisée bombée**   round head
    countersunk screw (decorative, used with
    cup washer)

~ **à tête ronde**   round head screw

~ **à tête six pans**   Allen (hexagonal) socket
    head screw

~ **auto perceuse**   self-tapping screw

~ **Phillips®**   Philips® screw

~ **Pozidrive / Pozi**   Pozidrive screw

~ **sans tête**   grub screw

~ **tire-fond tête hexagonale**   coach screw

~ **trompette**   drywall screw (for plasterboard)

---

vis *n(f)* **sans tête**   grub screw
viser *v*   to screw (fix)
visiter *v*   to view (property)
visiteur (trice) *n(m)/(f)*   viewer (of property)
visserie *n(fpl)*   fixings (bolts and screws)
visseuse *n(f)*   powered screwdriver
vitrail (aux) *n(m)*   stained glass window
vitre *n(f)*   window pane
vitré *adj*   glazed (window etc)
vitrer *v*   to glaze (window etc)
vitres *adj* **(sans ~)**   unglazed (window, door)
vitrier *n(m)*   glazier
vitrine *n(f)*   window (shop, display)
voie *n(f)* **d'accès**   service road
voie *n(f)* **respiratoire**   airway *n* (for breathing)
voisin *adj*   adjoining (room)
volet *n(m)*   shutter
volige *n(f)*   batten (roofing)
volt *n(m)*   volt

Voltmètre   Vue

voltmètre *n(m)* voltmeter
volume *n(m)* volume (cubic space)
voûte *n(f)* vault (roof)
voûté *adj* vaulted
voûtés *n(fpl)* vaulting (ceiling)
voyant *n(m)* light indicator (on switch,
appliance)
vrac *adj* **(en ~)** loose (material / items not pre-
packed)
vrille *n(f)* auger (for timber)
vrillette *n(f)* death watch beetle; furniture
beetle
vue *n(f)* view (scenery)

Wassingue   White spirit

wassingue *n(f)* spokeshave
watt *n(m)* watt (elec.)
wattmètre *n(m)* wattmeter
white-spirit *n(m)* white spirit

Zinc

zinc *n(m)* zinc (metal)

About the Editor

Property restoration has played a central role in William Rees' varied career. In 1971 he was one of the principals of a family company that purchased Glansevin - a small mansion in Carmarthenshire. In that capacity he supervised the complete rebuilding of one wing dating from the 17th century together with major works elsewhere. Subsequently a Georgian property in nearby Llandeilo required refurbishing throughout. In 2000 he moved to France and purchased a village farmhouse in la Vienne which was extensively renovated by his own efforts.

Otherwise William has devoted much of his life to the media and to the leisure industry. After training in journalism and working in news and current affairs with Independent Television he established a company producing documentary material principally for S4C Wales. He was a columnist with the South Wales Evening Post for 17 years.

Glansevin had been developed as a country hotel and theme restaurant. The parallel interests in writing and catering led William to free-lance in the field and contribute general material and restaurant reviews to the regional and trade Press. In 1995 he was the Overall Winner of the UK Year of Literature Food Writing Award. Subsequently, while in France, he contributed numerous reports from Poitou-Charentes, Limousin and Vendée to the Charming Restaurant France Guidebook.

Further copies of:

Will's DIY Dictionary
From Sewage to Shocking Pink

Premier (Review) Edition
October 2008.

This short-run Edition has been prepared
primarily for presentation to media sources
and wholesale booksellers. Nevertheless a
limited number are available for general sale.

At the moment they can only be supplied
directly from the Publisher on receipt of a
cheque for the appropriate amount. The First
Edition (late October 2008) will be available
through all good booksellers and the
Publisher – both directly and via the internet.

The Editor will be glad to sign and dedicate
any copies of the Premier (Review) Edition
purchased provided relevant instructions
accompany the payment.

Further copies
are available direct from:
Will's DIY Dictionary,
3 Waterloo Terrace, Carmarthen SA31 1DG
Wales. UK

Prices: UK (Inc. 1st Class letter post): £14.95
France: (By letter post).
(UK Sterling Cheques): £15.95
(French Euro Cheques); €18.95
(Copies will be despatched within one working day
of receipt of order (with cheque). When the Edition
is exhausted clients will be advised by e-mail or
contacted on a land-line telephone number.

More information on: www.Dadani.co.uk

Europe wide emergency –
☎ 112
(Access to English speaking operators).
France Medical Emergency – ☎ 15

emergency cas d'urgence
accident accident
fire feu; (major) incendie

my husband mon mari **my wife** ma femme
my son mon fils **my daughter** ma fille
my friend mon ami (e) *(m)/(f)*
a boy un garçon **a girl** une jeune fille
someone ... quelqu'un ...
... is injured ... est blessé
..is seriously injured ..est grièvement blessé
bone(s) os (singular & plural)
...has broken a bone / bones (in the ...)
...a cassé un os / les os (de ,,,)
a wound (to the ...) une blessure (au / à la..)
there's bleeding il y a saignement
heavy bleeding hémorragie
a burn une brûlure
he / she has had an electric shock
il / elle a pris une décharge électrique

we have had ... nous avons eu ...
...an accident with ... ...un accident avec ...
... a sharp tool ... un outil tranchant
... a power tool ... un outil électrique
...things have fallen ...les choses ont tombé
... a wall has fallen ... un mur a tombé
he / she is trapped il / elle est coincé

I have fallen down j'ai tombé
he /she has fallen down il / elle a tombé
... from the ladder / on the staircase
...dans l'échelle / dans l'escalier
he / she is breathing il / elle respire
... is not breathing ... ne respire pas